Six Keys
To Unlock the
Power of Prayer

Alice R. Cullinan

To a fine christian Joyce, Thank you for everything you do to help others in need, and making meals and having wonderful talks and laughter, you fine wheel chairs, table and chairs you take others to doctor can. help when-ever you Thank you for being my friend. You are loved + prayed for Dot

Revelation chp 3 v 20
June 15th 2022

Copyright © 2019 Lamplighters Ministries

All rights reserved.

ISBN:9781704358284

LampLighters Ministries
104 Annies Circle
Shelby. N.C. 28152

http://www.lamplighters-ministries.org
lamplightersministries@gmail.com

All rights reserved. No part of this publication may be translated, reproduced, or transmitted in any form or by any means, electronic or mechanical, including photocopy, recording, or any informational storage and retrieval system, without permission in writing from the authors, except for brief quotations included in a review of the book.

Bible quotations in this volume are from:

The Holy Bible: New International Version, copyright 1973, 1978, 1984. Used by permission of Zondervan Bible Publishers. All rights reserved.

The Holy Bible: Amplified Version, copyright 1954, 1958, 1964, 1987 by the Lockman Foundation. All rights reserved. Used by permission.

The Holy Bible: New American Standard Version, copyright 1995 by the Lockman Foundation. All rights reserved. Used by permission.

Acknowledgements

Special thanks to my family and friends who helped with this project through words of encouragement, by reading the manuscript to suggest ways to make concepts clearer, and for their willingness to be involved in the meticulous process of finding typographical and grammatical errors. I appreciate them for what they did to make this book as helpful and error-free as possible. Some of those who helped in this project were:

My brother, Jim, who spent hours editing and re-editing the manuscript, and making suggestions about where the concepts needed to be clearer.

My friends, Lisa Barbee, Elaine Ashley, and Martha Fraser, for being willing to read the manuscript for typing errors, and for their support and prayers as I wrote the book. Martha also prodded me to write the book, and was willing to conduct opinion polls at her church regarding the topics that I should include.

My friends and prayer supporters, Dee Tillett and Ann Scism, for their prayers and encouragement in the entire process.

For those who were willing to share with me what prayer means to them, a synopsis of which I have placed in the appendix of this book.

And, of course, I want to acknowledge the leadership of God's Spirit in the entire process...of teaching me about prayer as well as helping me put on paper some of the things that He has taught me.

Table of Contents

Acknowledgements 3

Introduction 7

Key 1: Have a Clear Understanding of Prayer 9

Key 2: Your Prayer-Life Must Be Well-Balanced 39

Key 3: Understand the Role of the Scripture in Prayer ...65

Key 4: Study Jesus' Prayer Life and Instructions 95

Key 5: Understand the Role of the Holy Spirit 123

Key 6: Learn How to Listen to God 141

Conclusion 177

Appendix Materials:

1. Spiritual Inventory 181

2. God's Promises and How to Claim Them..................189

3. Testimonies about Prayer 197

Introduction

Most people pray at one time or another, whether they are Christians, people of other faiths, or even non-religious individuals. There seems to be something within us all that causes us to reach out to some kind of Higher Power, especially during times when life feels overwhelming. Some people pray daily, while others only pray when life is difficult. Some people believe that praying is simply a religious ritual or a way to ensure future happiness. Others find their prayers to be comforting, renewing, and inspiring. Some engage in prayer because they were taught that it is important; while others believe that such religious activity will earn favor with a Supreme Being.

Since there are literally hundreds of books published about prayer, you may wonder why I decided to write another one. I believe that no matter how much we study prayer, and no matter how often we actually pray, the topic can never be exhausted. Our God is too big (and a potential relationship with Him is too vast), for one book to be able to include everything about prayer. The wonderful blessings that He wants to give to us, His children, are too numerous to name and often too difficult to grasp. We need a great deal of help to learn what prayer is all about, and how to do it more effectively.

When I first decided to write this book, I wanted to be sure that I made it as practical and applicable as possible. I first wrote a list of what I think are the most important things for us to know and do, in order for our prayer life to be one of great joy and effectiveness. I am calling these necessary steps 'keys,' because I believe that they are the tools by which the power of prayer is unlocked.

It is my hope and prayer that you will use these six 'keys' to help you access the power of prayer in your own life. Prayer is too often an untapped source of strength and power, a reservoir of faith-growth that we often fail to access. Connecting to God through prayer brings immeasurable joy, godly wisdom, hope, peace and strength.

- Alice Cullinan

Key 1:

Have a Clear Understanding of Prayer

The topic of prayer is vast... one that will take all of our lives to even begin to grasp. Its purpose and power, and how God designed for us to be a vital part of His ministry in our world, are truths that are sometimes difficult for mere mortals to understand. We can gain valuable insight as we consider both the first prayers that a young child utters at bedtime, and the powerful communication with God by the seasoned saint who goes boldly to God's throne of grace. One of the first hurdles that we must face, however, is our limited and/or misinformed understanding of what prayer really is. We often have the erroneous concept that prayer is mainly asking God for what we want Him to do for us or someone else. The true breadth and purpose of prayer will take a lifetime of learning, but hopefully what I share with you in this book will be helpful to you as you seek to deepen your relationship with God through prayer.

What is Prayer?

Perhaps the simplest way to understand prayer is to realize that it is *communication with God that includes talking, listening, and enjoying His presence*. It is the method by which we tap into the power and presence of God for ourselves and for others. Prayer is not learning how to SAY the appropriate words for God (and others) to hear. When I was a new Christian, I was confused about this truth. I wanted to learn how to pray correctly, to 'say the right things in the right way', so that God would answer my prayers. I first listened to what others were saying in their prayers, and I tried to learn some of the words and phrases that I heard them say. I also read as many books as possible on the topic. One summer, a friend and I decided to get together to practice praying correctly. We believed that this would help us learn how to pray effectively. As we listened to other people voice their requests to God in prayer, we noticed the repetition of many prayer 'phrases.' We concluded that it must be important to repeat these phrases.

As I look back on my journey of learning how to pray, I have to smile. During those early days of my life as a new Christian, the King James Version of the Bible was popular. Prayers usually included the use of *Thee* and *Thou*, *Shalt* and *Wilt*, and other words used by that version of the Bible. But it was awkward for me, a new Christian, to learn a new way of talking! It felt more spiritual to me, however, if I prayed with those words. It was my firm belief that no one would ever want to address the King of the Universe with such words as You and Yours! Many years have gone by since those early days of my walk with Jesus. I have read many books on prayer, as well as diligently studied what the Bible teaches on the subject. My understanding of prayer has changed tremendously. But, as most people will discover at some point along their prayer journey, we learn the most about prayer by actually praying. It is this 'lab work' that teaches us the most! As we walk with Jesus, read His word, learn to talk and listen to Him, and see how He answers prayer, our understanding grows.

Looking at Prayer in a Different Way

One day, while I was working on a devotional guide on prayer, I tried to think of a way to express a concept on prayer that I felt would be helpful for those who read it. I wanted people to realize that prayer is simply walking with and talking/listening to a friend. He is the One with Whom we share our joys and concerns. I came up with the following list of helpful ways to think about prayer:

Prayer is:

-walking and talking with a friend who wants to know how we are doing.

-a time of unburdening to our Counselor, and listening for His advice.

-a time of seeking truth from our Teacher, and then obeying it with all of our hearts.

-a time of talking with the Compassionate One about others who need a blessing from Him.

-a time of seeking guidance from our Guide as we walk the journey of life.

-a time of openness, honesty, and confession when we have sinned and gone our own way.

-a time of sharing our sorrow with the only One who can bring healing and wholeness.

-a time to tap into divine strength for our needs, and receive the necessary power to accomplish His will.

-a time to bask in the light of His presence in order to dispel our own darkness.

-a time to breathe in His power, letting go of our worry, control and weaknesses.

-a time to receive what He wants to give to us, and to give Him our lives in return.

-a time to hear His words of love, especially when we are feeling unlovely.

-a time to praise and thank Him for who He is, as well as for what He has done.

-a time to escape the pain of loneliness, by drawing closer to the One who is always with us.

Which of these descriptions of prayer speak to you today? Which ones of them have you never considered before now? Which ones will you try to include in your prayer life? Will you try to change your perspective on prayer from merely words that you say, to a time when you fellowship with the Lord?

Practicing the Presence of God

Many years ago, Brother Lawrence wrote a book entitled <u>The Practice of the Presence of God.</u> It was his personal testimony of how he learned to talk with God, and to consciously be aware of His presence, even while he washed dishes in the monastery where he was a monk. I read his book and decided that I would make a commitment to never let a day go by that I did not do whatever it took to be aware of the sweet presence of the Lord. It has been a delight to keep that commitment! I challenge you to do the same thing, and will offer a few suggestions on how to do that. Walking and talking with God, as well as feeling His presence and listening to what He wants to say to us, is the essence of what prayer is all about. Here are a few things that have helped me:

1. The first thing to do is to make the decision to seek to connect with God each day. I personally find it easier to do this in the morning, before I get involved and distracted with other responsibilities. However, if that schedule does not work for you, find some time when you can focus on your relationship with God.

2. Read the Bible, asking the Holy Spirit to help you to connect with God and to hear His voice. Whenever you read the Bible, your reaction should be like it would be if you read a letter from a loved-one. You would probably read it slowly, thinking about where the person was they wrote the letter, how they were feeling when they wrote it, etc. But sometimes we respond like we do when we get a bill in the mail. We know that we should see what the envelope contains, but we really don't want to know! Unfortunately, at times we are like that when we open the Bible. We know the 'news' inside is something we need, but we aren't sure we are really ready to hear it! We are guilty of rushing through our Bible readings, instead of letting the words connect us to the Lord, mentally and spiritually.

3. Ask the Lord to help you connect to Him, to help you hear His voice and sense His presence. Talk with Him in a conversational tone. Prayer is a talk with a friend, not a research paper that we are reading to our professor!

4. Use music to help you connect to the Lord. Music touches our spirits. You should select music that says something about the presence of the Lord, about His love for you. As the words are coupled with the music, it often will bring a sense of His presence to you. You can also sing the words that say to Him how much you love and need Him.

5. Use your imagination to help you connect to the presence of God. For instance, invite Him to sit beside you in the car when you are driving. Imagine that He is sitting there with you. Talk with Him like you would any other passenger. Of course, it is better to do this when you are in the car alone!

6. If you enjoy talking on the phone, use it while pretending to talk with God. Again, it is probably best if you are in the room alone. If anyone catches you doing this activity, you can refer them to this part of the book as a way to keep them from being extremely worried about you!

It is necessary for you to focus mentally when you are seeking to be aware of God's presence. Recall His promises to always be with you, and imagine that He is beside you. Or, you may find it helpful to imagine that He is in heaven, with His glory shining down on you like sunshine does. You can lift your head toward heaven, as you would enjoy the rays of the sun, and tell Him how much you love Him and appreciate His presence with you.

Sometimes, the Lord will surprise you with a sense of His presence, even when you are busy doing something that has completely occupied your mind at the time. And there are times when you sense God's presence and realize that it might be because someone is praying for you. Whether you know what is going on or not, enjoy His presence and share your heartfelt love with Him.

There are inspirational stories shown at the end of many of the evening news casts on TV. I like to watch them, since they are a welcomed relief after twenty-five minutes of bad news! They provide inspiration, sometimes bringing viewers like me to tears. In one story recently, a soldier who came home on leave from an overseas assignment had not let family members know about his planned visit. When they entered their home, they were overjoyed when they saw their loved-one. Such it is with us at times: God surprises us, showing up when we least expect Him! Even though we do not have any control over those 'surprise visits,' we do have some control over the day-by-day times when we focus on and appreciate His sweet presence. Please don't fail to make a commitment to make these times the rule and not the exception!

The Friend with Whom We Want to Walk

Throughout our lives, we learn that friends are treasures. They help us navigate life and are there for fun, as well as during times of distress. But we sometimes discover that some friends can betray us, disappoint us, fail to be there for us, or can be a tremendous source of pain and disillusionment. Because we are hurt from time to time by our friends, such experiences can make us less likely to open up to someone else. We have been hurt, so we don't want to trust anyone again. We had shared our lives and even our secrets with them...but they betrayed us.

As I look back over my own life, it is eye-opening when I remember how certain friends were or were not there for me. I realize how my trust-level has been hurt or helped by their reactions to me. It was the betrayal by a co-worker, when I was only nineteen (and still not a Christian), that caused me to seriously consider committing suicide. Thankfully, God sent me to someone else who won me to faith in Jesus, and then became a wonderful friend!

Many of us know the hymn, "What a Friend We Have in Jesus." It is a reminder to us of the faithful friendship of the Lord. But there are some people who have been disappointed in God, because they felt that He betrayed them, or at least had let them down. They became disillusioned with God when He did not answer a prayer. Or they were hurt by a professing Christian, or their faith was shattered when a trusted pastor chose to be immoral. And when church members act in a hypocritical manner, claiming to know and love God while living a sinful lifestyle, some people's faith is hurt. They begin to think that Christianity is all a farce.

Before our prayer lives can be both effective and enjoyable, it is urgent to remind ourselves of who God is, who Jesus is, and who the Holy Spirit is. We need to believe that the entire Trinity is trust-worthy, loving, and reliable. We must grow to understand just how much they love us and want to spend time with us, before we will want to do the same with them. What is your concept of God? Have your beliefs about Him been influenced in a positive or negative manner because of your own father? What about Jesus? What is your concept of Him? Do you know that He loves to spend time with you, and that He wants to become your best friend? What about the Spirit? Do you simply think of Him as a feeling or something else intangible? Do you realize that He also wants to bless you, to guide you, to comfort you, and to help you learn how to pray?

Do you believe that it brings joy to the heart of God to bless you, to walk with you, and to help you? Do you realize that He wants you to be a blessing to others through prayer? Do you think of prayer as something you "DO" or "SAY" rather than being a fun walk with a friend? I suggest that you periodically ask and answer these questions, since it is important for you to have the proper perspective on your relationship with God, as you study how to be more proficient in prayer.

Why Should We Pray?

One day, after a class I was teaching at the university, one of the college students stayed to ask a question. "Dr. C," he said, "Why should we pray? God knows what we need, and will do what He wants to do, whether or not we pray." I talked with him about his concept of prayer, and about a few things that I felt he should keep in mind about prayer. I shared with him that prayer is not just simply asking God to do something for us or for someone else. When we have a limited understanding of what prayer really is, we cheat ourselves out of many blessings.

Unfortunately, our times of prayer are often relegated to Sundays, repeating a blessing at mealtimes, or when we are in great difficulty and needing God's help or healing. But is this really all that we should expect from prayer? What do you think are some of the reasons for spending time in prayer? There are many reasons to pray, but perhaps the following are some of the most important ones.

1. **Prayer is a chief way to enhance our relationship with God**. None of us would expect to grow in a particular human relationship without spending time with the person. So, why do we think we can get to know God better without having regular times of talking and listening to Him? Some of the greatest bonds are formed between people by simply hanging out together. Haven't we realized how important it is to focus on simply being with God? When we recognize His presence with us, and understand that He wants to enjoy what we enjoy, it can be quite a boost to our prayer life! One of the barriers many people erect between themselves and God is falsely believing that God expects us to say the right thing in the right way before He will answer. They focus on having the correct words, while sometimes overlooking the need to simply share what is on their hearts with the One who loves them completely.

2. **God has designed prayer as a way to change us and others**. When we learn how to tap into God's power through prayer, it will change us. And when we learn how to tap into this power of God and become a channel of blessing to others through intercession, it will change both them and us! We don't have to understand how all of this works before we can benefit from it. I have no idea how electricity works, but this does not keep me from using it to have power for what I need.

3. **God accomplishes His purposes in this world through the prayers of His people**. He invites us to work with Him to bless us and this world. How sad it is when we "*do not have, because we do not ask.*" (James 4:2-3). It is equally sad if we remain weak when His strength is available. (2 Cor. 12:9-10) And how tragic it is when the lost are not reached, because we do not '*pray and ask the Lord of the harvest to send laborers into His harvest.*'(Mt. 8:37-38)

God wants to bless us and use us to bless others. He wants us to be a channel through whom His Spirit can work. We are an extension cord, tapping into the ultimate power source through prayer, releasing His power to flow through us to others.

What Prayer is NOT

In our quest to understand prayer, we must keep in mind that prayer is NOT what we (and others) at times may have made it out to be. Consider the following erroneous concepts.

1. **Prayer is NOT talking God into doing something**. Many people think that it is necessary to beg God to do something, by presenting enough compelling reasons to force Him to do what we want. Or, we believe that enlisting enough people to join us in praying will obligate God to grant our requests. This is NOT what prayer is! God wants to bless His children more than we could ever imagine. We must realize that He, and He alone, knows what is best for us. He can be trusted to do what is right, what is beneficial, what is going to promote kingdom values. He never makes mistakes, never willfully refuses to give to His children what is best for them. When we can accept these truths about God's person and

motives, it frees us to live in childlike trust. Our prayers will more likely be ones of praise and gratitude, when we realize just how much He loves us and wants the best for us.

2. **Prayer is NOT just a wish-list of desires to present to God to grant/accomplish.** God is not a spiritual vending-machine into which we place a prayer, and out comes a prize. Although petitions are an acceptable form of prayer, even our petitions must be ones that are God-honoring. (In Key 2, we will discuss the various types of prayers, and why and how they are acceptable to God.)

3. **Prayer is NOT just feeling better because we talk something over with someone who loves us.** Of course, we will feel relieved after we unload a burden onto God, but just wanting to feel better is not the reason for praying. We pray because we know that God cares for us, and wants to help us with whatever difficulty we may be facing. He is our best friend, you know! But He is more than just a friend. He is the King of the Universe, the mighty Creator who made us. He is our Shepherd; we are His sheep. He knows what is best for us, and what His will is for us. He knows why He has allowed or sent a test into our lives. He knows when and how we need to be taught to walk the right path with Him. He knows how easy it is for us to stray away from Him. He cares. He loves. He lifts our burdens. He guides. He comforts. He teaches. Why would we NOT want to spend time in His presence?

Be Sure That You Are On 'Praying Ground'

Hebrews 4:16 tells us to *'approach the throne of grace with boldness, in order to receive mercy and find grace to help us in our time of need.'* The only reason we can do this is because of our relationship with Jesus. We must *'hold firmly to the faith we profess,'* and we are able to do so because we have a *'sympathizing high priest,'* our Savior. But we must never take this invitation to pray, to *'approach the throne of grace boldly,'* as a matter of pride or entitlement. Our hearts must be humbled before our Mighty God. But we must also realize that we are children of the King; those who have been adopted into His family, because of the atoning sacrifice of Jesus. Presumption has no rightful place in the mind and heart of a child of God. Yet, we are summoned to walk with a holy God, and to converse with Him about everything on our hearts. How can we live up to our responsibility in the matter of effective prayer? We have to be "on praying ground"...holy and cleansed. This is the only way we can expect to be able to stand before the King of the Universe. We must be properly prepared before we attempt to meet with the Lord. We know that He is our Father, but we must never forget that He is Almighty God.

God called out of a burning bush to His servant Moses, but as Moses walked toward the bush, God spoke again: *"Don't come any closer. Take off your sandals, for the place where you are standing is holy ground."* (Ex. 3:5) Even though it was God who initiated the encounter, Moses was instructed to come humbly into the presence of a holy God. In a sermon he preached in 1871, the famous preacher, Charles Spurgeon said:

"We are still on **praying ground** and pleading terms with God, and the throne to which we are bidden to come, and of which we speak at this time, is the throne of grace. It is a throne set up on purpose for the dispensation of grace, a throne from which every utterance is an utterance of grace; the scepter that is stretched out from it is the silver scepter of grace; the decrees proclaimed from it are purposes of grace; the gifts that are scattered down its golden steps are gifts of grace; and He that sits upon the throne is grace itself. It is the throne of grace to which we approach when we pray..."[1]

There are two small dogs living at my house...correction: I live at their house! At least, they act in charge, most of the time. They obviously know that they have me wrapped around their paws. But there are times when I have to deal with their errors, to let them know who is in charge of them. One of those times is when they go out into the yard after it has rained. After traipsing through the wet grass, and walking on the red clay dirt, they come to the door to be let inside once again. But, when I notice that their feet are covered with red dirt, I gently pick them up and take them to the kitchen sink for a quick foot-wash. They must be cleansed before they can have 'full fellowship with me and my beige carpet!' Do they like the process? Not at all. But it is necessary, if they want to be allowed back into my house and presence. I don't fuss at them for what happened to them, unless they decide to once again play and dig in the mud! But, whether they meant to get dirty or not, cleansing is a requirement for 'full-fellowship' with me.

Such it is with us and God. If we want to have full fellowship with Him and full access to prayer power, then cleansing must occur. I must submit to His conviction and His willingness to 'cleanse me from all unrighteousness,' as I

---

[1] "The Throne of Grace," a sermon preached by Charles Spurgeon on Nov. 19, 1871. (biblbb.com)

confess my sin. (I John 1:9) Then I will find myself once more 'on praying ground.'

My pups might decide that they don't like being isolated from me because of their dirty paws…but remain unwilling to come to me for the 'kitchen-sink wash-job.' As long as they run from me, they will remain away from close fellowship with me. Hopefully, we are not content to remain away from an intimate relationship between us and our Heavenly Father.

Some Prerequisites for Powerful Praying

Because the Lord ordained that prayer should be a vital part of the Christian's life, He knows what we need to do in order to be positioned for effective prayers. There are requirements to meet before we can walk and talk with a Holy God. Alexander Pope, in his poem *An Essay on Criticism* wrote, "Fools rush in where angels fear to tread." It would be good for us to remember this truth! We want to have power in prayer, to be able to conduct business with the King of the Universe. But we sometimes forget that we must be prepared before we can expect to walk and talk with God. He is Holy, and we are not. He has set up criteria for us humans to meet, if we want to have open communication and fellowship with Him. He has established these prerequisites, and we would be wise to understand and obey them!

The Bible is our guide, of course, so we will look at some of the *instructions* which it provides on how to be prepared to pray. 2 Chronicles 7:14 is a good place to begin.

> *If my people, who are called by my name, will humble themselves and pray and seek my face and turn from their wicked ways, then I will hear from heaven, and I will forgive their sin and will heal their land.* (NIV)

1. If we want free and open access to God, and expect Him to hear and to answer our prayers, the **first thing we must have is a humble heart and attitude**. Humility is defined in Webster's Dictionary as 'a modest or low view of one's importance.' It is the opposite of pride and arrogance. Romans 12:3 says *"Do not think of yourself more highly than you ought, but rather think of yourself with sober judgment, in accordance with the faith God has distributed to each of you."* There are many examples in the Bible of people who were proud, and God failed to answer their requests. But there are also many accounts of humble people who successfully entreated God, who granted their heart's desire.

2. **In addition to humility, we have to actually pray.** It is amazing how often people desire God's leadership or blessing, but still fail to ask Him for them! God expects us to ask, seek and knock. (Matt. 7:7). It is not sufficient simply to wish something or think about something. We need to PRAY.

3. **Another prerequisite for effective prayer is seeking God's face.** *"Seek the LORD while he may be found; call on him while he is near."* (Is. 55:6) *"...for the LORD searches every heart and understands every desire and every thought. If you seek him, he will be found by you...."* (I Chron. 28:9) Jesus Himself taught the importance of continuing to seek God. (Matt. 7:7). We must do everything

possible to connect with God, if we want to be successful in our prayers.

4. God also expects us to turn from our wicked ways. Why is it so easy for us humans to believe that it really does not matter how we are living? We think that God will have pity on us and answer our prayers, no matter what kind of lifestyle we are living! This is probably one of the chief obstacles to an effective prayer life…failing to live the kind of life which God has ordained for us to live. We need to remember what the psalmist shared: *"Who may ascend the mountain of the LORD? Who may stand in his holy place? The one who has clean hands and a pure heart, who does not trust in an idol or swear by a false god."* (Ps. 24:3-4)

Most of us would never describe our own behaviors or attitudes as 'wicked.' It sounds like such an extreme definition of behavior which is surely not true of us. But, it is important for us to understand that *any* sin or disobedience is considered wicked in God's sight. Being obedient, and confessing our sins when we are disobedient, are important prerequisites for connecting with God in prayer. (You should take a few moments to complete the following spiritual inventory to help you realize how easy it is for us to be 'wicked.')

Taking a Look at Ourselves

God's Spirit, who dwells within us, can be grieved or quenched by us. **Circle** the following 'prayer-blockers' that you need to confess (and have Him cleanse) in order for you to be a useable vessel, one who is 'on praying ground.' (Think back over the past week. Most of us cannot consider a longer time-frame without becoming overwhelmed with our own humanity!)

Mind:

Love of human praise   Pessimistic   Resentful

Stubborn   Impure thoughts   Egotistical

Proud in one's own accomplishments   Selfish ambition

Confusion   Prayerlessness   Judging others

Revengeful   Disobedient   Hotheaded   Negative

Irritable   Stressed   Unforgiving   Selfish

Doubting   Unthankful   Mean-spirited

Eyes: Ears:

Lust   Envy   Greed   Listened to gossip

Attuned to criticism   Closed to spiritual truths

Mouth/tongue:

Criticism of others   Profanity   Boasting   Lying

Rudeness   Foolish Joking   Quarreling   Devoid of praise

Grumbling   Hypocritical   Godless chatter

Complaining   Slander   Dirty jokes   Harshness

Too talkative   Insincere   Dishonest

Heart:

Discouraged   Depressed   Full of hatred

Lonely   Little enthusiasm   Touchy   Angry

Hostile   Arrogant   Temper (short fuse)

Unloving   Uncompassionate   Impatient   Anxious

Negative attitude   Worried   Fearful   Guilt   Shame

Tense   Nervous   Bitterness   Disgusted   Apathetic

Deceitful   Lazy   Rebellious

List anything else that the Lord may have brought to your mind that should be confessed, cleansed and removed from your life. Is there anyone you need to forgive, or to ask to forgive you?

Rate Your Spiritual Temperature for the Past 6 months:

___Hot   ___Cold   __Lukewarm   __Changeable

Be conscientious about keeping your sins confessed and cleansed, and you will find that your prayer life will be more effective, and your walk with God more joyful.

My Personal Reflections about Prayer

I have been a student and a practitioner of prayer for over sixty years. Some of my own ideas about prayer are as follows:

1. The relationship fostered *with* the Lord through prayer is more beneficial than any joy we may feel from a request granted *by* the Lord. Of course, Jesus instructed us to "*ask, seek, and knock.*" (Matt. 7:7) He also said: "*...how much more will your Father in heaven give good gifts to those who ask him.*" (Matt. 7:11) It is normal for us to ask God to do what we want Him to do, to show us what we need to see, and to give us what we think we need. But the real joy in prayer is our relationship with the Father Himself. Some of my fondest memories are when I was able to spend quality time with my earthly father. Whether it was learning how to repair a lawnmower, going with him to a men's Bible class, singing around the piano in our living room, or working together on a math problem...it was being WITH him that was the real blessing. We really should feel the same way about our relationship with God in prayer. We want to be WITH our Father. It doesn't really matter what else we want to happen or to receive.

2. In our conversation with God, it is much more transforming when He speaks to us, rather than when we fill the time with all of our concerns and requests. Most of us are not good listeners. During conversations with others, we may be the one who does most of the talking, or we may be easily distracted by our own thoughts or plans. Some studies show that people spend about 55% of their communication each day in listening. But most people usually only remember about 17-25% of what they hear. A study reported in the Harvard Business Review states that the average person remembers only half of what he has heard, even when making a special effort to listen. [2]

The same thing is true in our relationship with God. I am not aware of any studies on how difficult it is to hear from God, but it stands to reason that it is even harder than listening to people. Perhaps this is why the Lord used various means to get the attention of His people. He used visions, angelic messengers, burning bushes, dreams, other people, written documents, and miracles as some of the many ways to speak to humans. (In the last chapter of this book, we will discuss ways to help us be better at listening to God. At this point in our study, I will simply say that it is important for us to realize the importance of doing it!)

3. Satan, and our old nature, will work unceasingly to disrupt our fellowship with God, even using religious activity and other 'good things' to replace time which should be spent with God Himself. Have you ever tried to talk to someone who was preoccupied with something else at the time? You may have asked them to 'stop what they were doing,' but they kept on working or cooking or texting someone. They may have even tried to assure you that they could do what they were doing and still listen to you. Some people might be successful at multi-tasking to some degree, but you probably felt ignored or demeaned. You may have concluded that what you wanted to say was not important to the person.

---

[2] Harvard Business Review, hbr.org.

I am certain that God often feels neglected because of the busy-ness of our schedule. We might even say a few words in prayer as we run out of the door to school or work. And we might take a few moments at bedtime to pray or read a passage of Scripture. But do we ever take time to listen...to seek to really hear from God? Do we ever think about the truth that having fellowship with us, and speaking to us, are really the main reasons that God created us? Do we realize how Satan is actively at work in our lives to disrupt and distract us, trying to keep us from spending time with God?

4. God's purpose for creating mankind was for us to experience a loving relationship with Him. This must be the primary focus in our prayer lives. This is why cleansing is so important in our relationship with a God of holiness. To allow iniquity, pride and/or an unforgiving spirit to linger in our hearts will rob us of the intimacy of the holy presence of God Himself. Recently, a former student came by the house to talk with me about some relationship problems he was experiencing. He felt alienated from a close friend, and he didn't know what to do. He mentioned his discussions with the person, and had apologized for anything he may have done to cause the alienation. But his friend would not reveal what had caused the breech in their close friendship.

God is indeed our best friend. But there are things we do or say which cause estrangement between us and God. He is holy...we do unholy things. He is perfect ... we are imperfect. But He will tell us where the problem is, if we ask Him ...and if we will listen. It is helpful to use a spiritual inventory[3] on a regular basis, to help us be on guard against things that come into our lives which disrupt our fellowship with God. When we read the Bible each day, the Spirit can use it to show us where we have failed, or where we need to change. God is a God of forgiveness and cleansing, but He also expects us to cooperate with His Spirit, and to *'yield our bodies as living sacrifices to Him, holy and pleasing to God.'* (Romans 12:1) We must not remain in a 'state of alienation' between us and our Best Friend.

5. When prayer degenerates into primarily a list of requests, it has fallen from its lofty place and has sunk into the pit of selfishness. It is both convicting and eye-opening to take time to write down our prayers. We can then go back and evaluate them to see how many of them would have to be described as 'selfish.' This is not to imply that we should never ask for anything for ourselves or our loved-ones. The Lord refutes such a mistaken concept in the model prayer (The Lord's Prayer), our guideline for praying properly. Even Jesus asked the Father to "let the cross pass from" Him. One safeguard to help keep us from wandering away from acceptable prayer requests into selfish ones can be seen in a passage in Luke 22. Jesus added to His prayer: *"Nevertheless, not what I want, but what You want." (Luke 22:42)* It is always safe to present your requests to God, but it is also important to add a phrase like this: *"I would like for You to grant this request, Father, but I want Your will to be done. I am willing to accept what You decide regarding my request."*

---

[3] See the Appendix of this book for a sample spiritual inventory.

6. Our attempt to manipulate God and/or circumstances through the means of prayer is simply another example of our need for His redemption from ourselves. In the heart of all people, I think, is the desire to be happy and to live a meaningful life. We don't just want to survive; we want to live. But there are many attempts to bring this about by ourselves. From our earliest infancy, we want to avoid pain, hunger, and loneliness. We want to be loved and needed, and to feel significant. We learn mostly from other people, and through trial-and-error. It dawns on us that some behaviors are more successful at bringing about our cherished, sought-after goals. When our attempts at happiness and pleasure, love and meaning, are successful, we usually repeat them. Change is hard, because there are many times when we do not want to risk leaving our 'safe-zones.' We develop 'control issues,' actions and reactions which have served us well in the past. They have helped us to remain somewhat stable and successful at reaching our goals. But this way of survival sometimes carries over into our relationship with God. We try to control Him...even through our prayers!

This type of 'spiritual control' is difficult to recognize, especially in ourselves. We believe that we are being humble...only to learn that we have become proud of our humility! We desperately need God's Spirit to control us...but we really don't want anyone, even God, to do that! Human nature is totally in need of redemption.

7. When we listen to our prayers, or become aware of the lack of them, it may be a good way to reveal what we actually believe about God. Several years ago, I taught a group study on prayer at a church where I was serving as part-time Minister of Education. I decided to have the group discuss some of the typical 'prayer phrases' used in corporate worship. "Lead, guide, and direct us;" "Be with us today;" and "Be with the missionaries," were some that were mentioned. Then I had the group decide whether the prayers were biblical or not. I laugh now as I remember their reactions, and what they said to me after the study. "Dr. C., you have totally messed up my prayer life! I have been asking the Lord to be with me, and tonight I realized that He is always with me. I don't need to pray that."

The group concluded that we should pray according to what we read and learn from the Bible, refusing to state our prayers only by what we hear others say. For instance, since God promised never to leave us nor forsake us, it is a wasted prayer to ask Him 'to be with us.' A better prayer would be to thank Him for always being with us.

After our study, we decided that most of our prayers will be prayers of thanks and praise. "Lord, thank You for the assurance that You are always with me. Help me to remember this, Father, whenever I am tempted to forget." You can pray, "Thank You for being with the missionaries whom You have called and sent out into the harvest fields. Please help them to be aware of Your presence, and please bless them and meet whatever needs they may have today."

8. "Be still and know that I am God" may be the best, but hardest, advice that God has given to us about prayer. Why is it so difficult for us humans: (1) to be still, and (2) to know (by practical experience) that God is God? Perhaps it is because it has been ingrained in us since infancy that we need to learn how to be independent, to make it in this world by our own strength and ingenuity. "Try harder." "Be smarter." "Be useful." "Figure it out." These are some of the phrases that were either ingrained into us with actual words, or we were influenced by the actions and examples of others who have been significant to us.

Adam and Eve were not the only humans who wanted to be as smart as God. One day, while I was thinking about some of my own interpersonal conflicts, it dawned on me that everyone really thinks they are right about most things! Whether we believe that our political party is 'the right one,' our doctrinal beliefs about God and the church are the correct ones, or our opinion about what brings true happiness is really a superior position…we believe that we are right. And the more volatile the topic, like religion or politics, the more likely these differences of opinion between people will escalate into real conflicts. We cannot all be right…but most of us think we are! So, why do I really need to 'be still before God, to get to know Him' in more profound ways? Obviously, I need His perspective on life and truth. And, when I do grasp God's perspective, how do I learn how to 'be still' before Him? (We will discuss these topics in more detail, later.)

9. If we are afraid to talk with God about anything, or we find ourselves afraid of His answers or reactions to our prayers, we are revealing our failure to understand just how much He loves us and wants intimate fellowship with us. One of my friends teases me sometimes, when I am trying to tell her something that she really doesn't want to hear. She will put her fingers in her ears and begin repeating 'la-la-la-la-la' as loudly as she can, attempting to drown out what I am saying. Her behavior reminds me of the behavior of children when they are afraid. They put their hands over their eyes to keep the OTHER person from seeing them!

Ignoring God by not praying is just one futile and hurtful way in which we reveal our inadequate beliefs about God. When we fail to confess our sins, we do not realize that we are scorning the sacrifice which Christ made on the cross... the one thing making forgiveness even possible. When we feel shame or guilt, but do nothing about it, we reveal a faulty belief that God's redemption is not readily available for humans. When we ignore Him, and fail to spend time with Him, we may be revealing that we are either heartless, or we do not realize the extent of God's love and desire to spend time with us.

10. How different our prayer lives would be if we were to focus on how we can bring joy to the heart of God, instead of requesting only a blessing from God. I wonder how different our lives would be if we asked our Lord what we could do for Him...instead of vice versa. "What can I do for You today, Lord? How can I bless You or Your children today?" Do you see that just this one change in perspective and focus could greatly alter our prayers... and our lives?

Not long ago, I decided to lead a study in my Sunday School class on the topic of "Pleasing God." We studied verses which specifically tell us things that please God. The study was actually very surprising. We also looked at verses about the things which displease God. (If I want to please Him, I need to stop doing what displeases Him!) It was amazing to me to realize the effect that this study had on me…on my perspective about life, and where my focus is in my prayers. I saw just how selfish my prayers really have been! I am so thankful that our loving Heavenly Father is patient with us. He often must say to us, whether we hear it or not: "Do you finally understand? It is fellowship with YOU that I want."

Why Don't Christians Pray More?

"If prayer is such a powerful tool, then why don't we do it more?" I remarked to my friend, Lisa Barbee, one day as we met for lunch. How would you answer that question? She and I came up with a list of reasons/excuses that many people give for not taking time to pray. Put a check mark beside the following ones that are true in your own life.

1. I don't think I have the time.

2. I don't think I know how to do it effectively.

3. I am not really sure that God answers prayers, unless they are for emergency situations.

4. I don't feel worthy enough to pray.

5. Life is just too busy and too stressful for me to focus.

6. I don't think God cares about daily, insignificant things.

7. I don't want to bother Him.

8. I don't think I should ask Him to do what I am capable of doing without Him.

9. I am not patient enough to wait for His reply, or I don't know how to hear what His answers are.

10. I have been disappointed in the past when He did not answer my prayers, or did not answer them like I wanted Him to.

How many of these 'reasons' for not spending time in prayer did you have to check? Take a few moments to think about why you don't spend much time in prayer. Do you feel guilty about any of your reasons? Are you willing to ask the Lord for His help in overcoming the obstacles in your life of prayer and fellowship with Him?

Here are a few questions that I think we should regularly ask ourselves, if we checked any of the above reasons for a lackadaisical prayer life.

1. Do I believe that there is anything more important than spending time with the One who died for me, who loves me completely, and who has the best plans possible to ensure my happiness?

2. Do I believe that God sent His Son to die for me, sent the Spirit to live inside of me, and has wonderful plans to bless and use me in His Kingdom? If I do believe these things, how can I forget His promise to do everything in His power to speak words of love and guidance to me, when I spend time talking and listening to Him?

3. Do I believe that my heavenly Father has promised never to forget me, that He will always love me, and that He will never be too busy for me to talk with Him about anything that is on my heart?

4. Does my heavenly Father require me to know exactly how to express my praise of Him or my requests to Him (in some kind of heavenly language) before my prayers are acceptable to Him? If my earthly parents and grandparents loved to hear my 'babbles of love' when I was an infant, do I think that my Heavenly Father expects me to know just how to express my prayers to Him, before He will do anything to answer them?

One morning in Sunday School, a class member shared about a visit that her young grandchildren made to her home. They spent the night, she said, and wanted to sleep in her bed with her. She went on to tell us, "I didn't get much sleep, because they were hugging me for most of the night. But I wouldn't have missed that experience for anything!"

What a wonderful glimpse of how God feels about us. He just wants us to hang out with Him, to love Him and to let Him love us. Whenever you wonder if you should spend time in prayer with the Lord, it is obvious that you need to reflect more on who He is, and how much He loves you. And it helps to read the Bible to help you understand the scope of His great love for His children. That activity alone should stir you to spend more time with Him! God's 'hugs' are something that you do not want to miss.

God desires to have a close relationship with us. He desires to provide our every need. But there are certain requirements which must be met before such a relationship between us and Him can occur. Prayer power is only available to bless us and others, when we follow the instructions.

Key 2:

Your Prayer-Life Must Be Well-Balanced

There are several *types* of prayers mentioned in the Bible. In order to have a well-balanced prayer life, we should be careful to include all of them. Of course, there will be times in our life when we may especially need strength from one specific type of prayer. Or there will be situations that we face when our joy is so full that our prayers will include praise and thanksgiving more than petition, confession, etc. But over a period of time, we should try our best to include all of the types of prayer in our communication with the Lord. Thankfully, in the Bible are instructions on how to do each of them effectively.

There is one word of warning, however. We must always avoid being so concerned about doing prayer right that it causes us to lose our focus on our relationship with the Lord. Consider how your communication with a loved-one can be adversely affected if you begin concentrating on HOW you are saying something, rather than just enjoying the time you are having with him/her. When we are praying, it should be a joyous time with our Lord. Of course, as with any human relationship, it is helpful to periodically think about some of the following: (1) Am I doing all of the talking, or none at all? (2) Am I listening carefully, trying to understand what I think that God is saying to me, or am I simply doing what I want to do? (3) Do I ever ask what God wants, or am I only telling Him what I want? (4) Do I care how He feels, or only about how I am feeling? (5) Do I enjoy being in His company, or do I want Him around only when I need something from Him? (6) Do I tell Him how I feel about Him, or do I just assume that He should know that? (7) Do I enjoy talking about Him with others, or do I fail to mention Him, unless asked? (8) Do I enjoy introducing Him to others, or do I ignore Him when I am with them?

These questions are some that we should ponder on a regular basis. A good way to discover what we think about prayer, that it is a relationship with God rather than things for which we ask Him, is to compare it with a relationship between us and a good friend or family member…and what it takes to make that relationship work well. *Prayer really is a relationship with God, not just a conversation.*

Enhancing our Relationship with God

There is a joke about an engaged man sharing an important message with his bride-to-be on their wedding day. The smiling man looks at his beautiful bride and says: "Honey. I want you to know something. I want you to know that I love you with all of my heart."

The beaming bride smiles back and says, "Oh, Darling. That is the sweetest thing that you could ever say to me."

The bridegroom then takes her by the hand and says, "And, Darling, I want you to always remember it... since this will be the last time I will tell you."

Is that acceptable behavior? Of course, it isn't. And we need to realize that there are some things that are *not* acceptable as far as our prayer-lives are concerned. Here are a few truths that we should glean from the illustration:

1. Prayer is indeed a relationship between us and our precious Loved-One. It is a relationship that must be nurtured as we walk with Him on a daily basis. We don't 'become wedded to Him,' and then leave Him at the altar.

2. Expressing our love to Him should NOT be limited to the time when we first became a Christian. It should be a repeated behavior, a huge part of praise and thanksgiving to Him, daily.

3. Our relationship with Him cannot grow stronger if we do not spend quality time with Him...talking, listening, and simply loving Him.

4. Coming to know Him better, and to love Him more, takes time and effort. It does not happen simply because we are growing older!

5. Talking ABOUT Him is not the same thing as spending time WITH Him. And no matter how much someone else knows Him and tells us about Him, it cannot replace the time that WE should spend with Him.

What are some of the ways you can get to know the Lord better and to grow in your relationship with Him? The most obvious thing, even before we look at some different types of prayer, is the fact that we must take time to be with Him! Spending time with Him, walking with Him, learning from Him, getting to know His likes and dislikes...over a period of time...will lead us into a closer relationship with Him.

On Facebook, there are often postings by spouses on birthdays and anniversaries. I often see these or similar words: "I love you more and more each passing year." That is a good description of what will happen when we learn to pray, to spend quality time with our Lord. We will come to love Him more each passing year. The words of one of my favorite hymns, written by Bill and Gloria Gaither, remind us of these truths.

> The longer I serve Him, the sweeter He grows,
> The more that I love Him, more love He bestows;
> Each day is like heaven, my heart overflows,
> The longer I serve Him, the sweeter He grows.

Types of prayer

There are many ways to communicate with God, of course, but there are some basic ones that we should try to include in our times of prayer. I will list the type of prayer, give a brief definition, an example of such a prayer in Scripture, and will then include an example of how you can express that type of prayer.

Praise: *Adoring God for who He is*. We should tell Him how much we love Him, how wonderful He is, how marvelous are the things He does, etc.

> *Bless (praise) the Lord, O my soul; and all that is within me, praise His holy name. Praise the Lord, O my soul, and do not forget any of all of His benefits.* (Ps 103:1-2)

O my blessed Lord, I praise You with all of my heart and soul. I praise Your name, O God, and lift my heart up to You in wonder and thanks. Help me never to forget even one small part of the many blessings that You give to me every day.

May my soul, from its deepest part, always express to You how I feel about You, and how truly grateful I am for everything.

Thanksgiving: *Expressing appreciation for what He has done for us, given to us and/or promised us.* A thankful heart deepens our love as quickly as anything can.

> *But thanks be to God! He gives us the victory through our Lord Jesus Christ.* (I Cor. 15:57)

Precious Father, how can I ever stop thanking You for all that You have done for me, and all that You mean to me? Thank You that I can approach the throne of grace because of what Jesus did for me. I come in His name with no merit of my own. Accept my love and my gratitude this day.

Confession: *Admitting our sin, repenting of it, turning from it and claiming God's forgiveness.*

> *Have mercy on me, O God, according to your unfailing love; according to your great compassion blot out my transgressions. Wash away all my iniquity and cleanse me from my sin. For I know my transgressions, and my sin is always before me. Against you, you only, have I sinned and done what is evil in your sight.* (Ps. 51:1-4)

Heavenly Father, I admit to You that I have sinned. I know that I break Your heart when I choose to go my own way. Thank You for Your willingness to forgive me and to cleanse me. Thank You for what Jesus did for me when He died on the cross. Help me, dear God, to walk in holiness and commitment to You. I repent of my sinfulness and stubbornness, and I claim Your forgiveness and cleansing of all of my sin.

Commitment: *Surrendering our will to the will of God.* Giving over to Him our decisions and choices, as well as placing upon Him anything that has distracted us from our relationship with Him.

> *"Abba, Father," he said, "everything is possible for you. Take this cup from me. Yet not what I will, but what you will."* (Mk. 14:36)

Father, You know what I don't want to be forced to experience right now in my life. You know the dread that I sometimes feel when I face difficulties. But, Father, I know that Your will is always best, and that Your grace is always sufficient. So, I place my life, my decisions and plans and desires into Your hands. I submit to Your will in everything.

Petition: *Specific requests.* Asking Him to do for us what we need, or to give to us our heart's desires.

> *This is the confidence we have in approaching God: that if we ask anything according to his will, he hears us. And if we know that he hears us—whatever we ask—we know that we have what we asked of him.* (I Jn. 5:14-15)

You know what is on my heart, dear Lord. I want Your will in it. I ask You for it, Lord, and know that Your answer is always the right one. Please grant my request, if it is in Your will, and will result in Your glory and my good. Thank You that I can trust you, whether the answer is 'Yes,' 'No,' or 'Wait.'

Supplication: *This is the 'Oh, help' prayer.* We do not even know what to ask for specifically, but we acknowledge that we need God and His help.

> *In my distress I called to the LORD; I cried to my God for help. From his temple he heard my voice; my cry came before him, into his ears.* (Ps 18:6)

Dear Father, sometimes I do not know what to say to You. I only know that I need Your help. I cry out to You for Your help and grace. I depend on You, Lord. I am in distress, but I really don't know all of the reasons why, or even what to ask You for. But Your grace is sufficient, so I will depend upon You.

Intercession: This is when we '*go between God and others,*' praying for them and their needs.

> *I urge, then, first of all, that petitions, prayers, intercession and thanksgiving be made for all people—* (I Tim. 2:1)

Dear Father, I gladly hold up to You in prayer those whom You have placed on my heart. Of course, I want to intercede for family and friends, but I also want to pray for our government leaders, for our missionaries who are spreading the word of God faithfully, for the sick and grieving, and for

Your will to be done in every believer's life. I also ask that You lay upon my heart those for whom You want me to intercede. And I want to thank You for the promise that both Jesus and the Holy Spirit are interceding for me.

Communion: Enjoying our time of fellowship with the Lord, simply *basking in and finding joy and comfort in His presence.* We don't have to talk at all.

> *We proclaim to you what we have seen and heard, so that you also may have fellowship with us. And our fellowship is with the Father and with his Son, Jesus Christ. We write this to make your joy complete. This is the message we have heard from him and declare to you: God is light; in him there is no darkness at all. If we claim to have fellowship with him and yet walk in the darkness, we lie and do not live out the truth. But if we walk in the light, as he is in the light, we have fellowship with one another, and the blood of Jesus, his Son, purifies us from all sin.* (I Jn. 1: 3-7)

Dear Lord, my heart's desire is to walk with You each day, to show You how much I love You, and to feel Your love in my heart. Show me if there is any darkness in my heart that is disrupting our relationship in any way, and I will gladly confess it and walk away from it. Your sweet presence and abiding love are what I am seeking each day.

Listening: This is when we are still before the Lord, waiting for Him to speak to us. And it should happen each time we open God's word to read it.

> *So, Eli told Samuel, "Go and lie down, and if he calls you, say, 'Speak, Lord, for your servant is listening.'" So Samuel went and lay down in his place. (I Sam. 3:9)*

Precious Father, I do want You to speak to me. I will be still and wait for You to say something to me. I will do whatever You say. My heart is filled with love for You. I want to spend time in Your presence, to express my love to You, and to hear what You would say to me.

Time to Reflect

How are you doing with these different types of prayer? Which are you neglecting, if any? Which are you over-utilizing? Which ones bring you the most comfort or enjoyment? Each of these different types of prayer can be used privately and publicly. Are you comfortable with all of these? How about when you are in public, or with just a few other people? Can you pray these ways without being self-conscious?

The Bible is filled with each of these types of prayer, and is a helpful tool in our quest to be more well-balanced in our own prayers. Consider the following Bible passages, and how the prayers are worded. You may find it helpful to pray these actual prayers while you are expanding your own prayer life. (I will also provide a differently worded version of the prayer which you may also want to pray, until you get comfortable using your own words.) Don't focus on just saying a prayer; focus on talking with your Father and your Savior. Try praying out loud, by yourself and with others, until you are comfortable praying in these different ways. It is important to remember, however, that God is more concerned with what is coming from your heart than how you are saying the words.

You may want to take some time each day to pray these types of prayer. You may want to write out some of them, as I have done here. If you focus on talking with the Lord, and not simply formulating some kind of acceptable prayer, your experience in prayer will be more meaningful and productive.

Praying the Names of God/Jesus

Understanding and calling on the names of God is another beneficial way to express our love and praise to the One who loves us completely. I find that when I do this, it makes certain prayers easier for me to pray. When I was a new believer in Jesus, I knew that it was important to praise and thank God. But I found out just how hard it was to do that! I knew that I could thank Him for my blessings, and that I was to praise Him for who He is; but when I tried it, my prayers were quite short! One day, I was introduced to a list of the names of God, with the challenge to use them when praying. What a difference this approach has made! I am going to share a few examples with you, hoping that you will be encouraged in your own prayer life to try some of them. If you find this approach helpful, there are many places where you can find information on the many names of God and Jesus.

Some of the Names of God:

***El Shaddai*: God Almighty**. You might pray something like this: Dear El Shaddai, I know that You are the Almighty King of the Universe. There is nothing too hard for You. There are no problems that I face that are too difficult for You to handle. Thank You for being my source of strength. I trust You to handle everything that concerns me today. I am weak, but You are not.

Jehovah Jireh: **The Lord will provide**. A possible prayer using this name: My precious Jehovah Jireh, I praise You. I can always count on You to provide whatever I need. Lord, whether it is personal, spiritual, or financial, You are there ready to provide for Your child. I praise You that You have never let me down. I know that You will never fail to give me what I need. Father, help me to learn to understand the difference between what I need and what I want. I know that I can count on You to always give to me what is best for me.

Jehovah Shalom: **The Lord is my peace**. Dear Loving Father, my Jehovah Shalom, You know how troubled I feel today. But I know that You care, and that You will always provide me with peace, because You are the God of peace. Help me to learn how to rely upon You today, and to willingly accept the peace that You want to give to me.

Adonai: **Master and Lord**. Dear Adonai, Your name brings me great comfort today. I have given my life to You, because You are Lord. It is not my responsibility to be in charge of my life; You are in charge. I humbly bow before You today, yielding all that I am, and all that I have to You. You are worthy, Lord, to be served and to be praised.

Father God: **This title stresses God's loving care, provision, and discipline**. My loving Father, thank You for adopting me into Your family. I feel great joy because I can always depend on You to care for me; I know that Your will is always best for me. I may not understand what You are allowing to happen in my life, and sometimes I cannot even feel Your presence. But I praise You for always being with me. I know that Your loving care will meet my every need.

Some of the Names of Jesus:

Shepherd of the Sheep: Dear Lord Jesus, how I praise You for being my shepherd. I feel like a lost sheep a lot of times, dear Lord. Life can hit me hard, and I often lose my way. But You are the good shepherd who cares for me. You lead me; You protect me; You find me when I stray. You forgive me and cleanse me, and comfort me when I am afraid or confused or depressed. How can I ever thank You for being my shepherd? Please accept my love, from a grateful heart.

Light of the World: Dear Jesus, I so often find myself in places of darkness. The world is a dark place. The darkness even infiltrates my heart at times, so much so that I despair of life itself. Then I remember that You are my light. When I come to You, You immediately dispel the darkness, and replace it with the light of Your loving presence. Thank You, from the bottom of my heart.

Water of Life: Dear Lord, life often drains me, and I feel so spiritually dry. But You are my living water. Thank You for giving me Your Holy Spirit, who is the river of life within me. Please help me to stop plugging up the flow of the river by my own fears, sin and disobedience. My lack of faith often is the main reason that my spiritual thirst is so overwhelming at times. You are my life. I praise You for that.

The Great High Priest: Dear Lord Jesus, I often feel the need for prayer and support. But many times, I do not know what to say, or I fear approaching the throne of grace for help. Thank You for being my Great High Priest, the One who is always interceding for me to the Father. Even when I fail to pray, or when others forget to hold me up in prayer, I know that You are always there. I can depend on You to faithfully minister to me, however and whenever I need it. I praise You, Lord. I thank You.

Immanuel: Dear Jesus, You know how terrifying it can be to be alone...really alone. Fears can be overwhelming, especially when people whom we thought we could count on have let us down. When there is such pain and the journey is a tough one, and even when others do not understand, I praise You that I can always count on Your presence, Your strength, and Your wisdom. You are with me. That is enough.

I hope you have seen by my prayers just how beneficial it can be to pray the names and attributes of God and Jesus. I also hope you will use this approach to help you in your own prayers. Read the prayers out loud until you feel comfortable talking with the Lord. Try writing out your prayers, since it can be an added blessing. At the very least, you should find time to talk with your Father! You will be blessed, as will He.

Using Music to Help Your Prayer Times

Have you ever stopped to realize that music is one of the few things here on earth that we will also enjoy in heaven? Music is a vital part of life, and it reaches to the innermost part of our mind and heart. Music has power to help us or to hurt us. It has tremendous power over our emotions, and words to songs can become pervasive in our thoughts.

Music attaches itself to memories, and sometimes its melodies can rob us of our sleep. But it also has the power to calm and soothe us, and to remind us of spiritual truths. It can transport us into the very presence of God, and is able to open our minds to truths that God's Spirit wants to convey to us. It helps us express our worship to God, and lifts our spirits to the throne of grace. It can usher us into the presence of God, challenge us to follow God closer, and convict us to the point that we are brought to tears. We must learn how to use music constructively in our prayer lives. I will share a few tips about how you can use music to help you pray.

1. Collect songs that speak to your heart, and which help you express your love and praise to God. Thankfully, there are many ways to find these helpful songs, without having to actually purchase them. Because I have been a Christian for many years, I have purchased music in many different formats. I have purchased vinyl records (of varying sizes), cassettes of various sizes, as well as CDs and DVDs. Now I use iTunes, Pandora, radio stations, YouTube, and other digital means to help me locate and buy songs that I can use to help me worship.

2. Since our spiritual and emotional needs vary from time to time, I suggest that you collect a variety of types of Christian music to use. Moods can be affected by songs, and vice versa. On certain days, you may feel the need to play songs which encourage you. At other times, you will want to play songs of repentance or praise.

3. Ask others to make recommendations of music that is helpful to use in prayer and worship. I have found, however,

that sometimes the songs that others suggest do not help me at all. Everyone has their favorite types of music.

4. Try experimenting with different types of music in order to broaden your prayer life. And find songs that express different kinds of prayer and worship. Be sure to include songs that are talking directly TO the Lord, as well as songs that are testimony songs ABOUT the Lord, His faithfulness, etc.

5. Use the hymnal as a way to pray. Find songs that are prayers to God, and either sing or say them out loud as your prayer. The book of psalms is the song book for the Israelites, so you may want to use it often as a way to pray and praise. You can even make up your own words to a tune that you know, or make up a melody to a psalm.

6. It is fun to make up your own song to sing to the Lord. It can be completely spontaneous with no structure or specific tune. Just use your voice as an instrument of praise and prayer. If you play an instrument, you can make up a tune and use it to worship the Lord.

7. Learn songs and their words, so that they can be playing in your mind and heart throughout the day. Select those which lift your spirit, or ones filled with the truth that you need for the day. I am always thankful when the Spirit starts playing a song in my heart. Sometimes, I awake in the morning with a song playing in my heart and mind.

8. As you do your Bible study, use a favorite psalm or other passage of Scripture. Take notes about why that passage is meaningful to you. Stop as you read a verse, and praise the

Lord for a certain truth, or use the passage to help you praise or intercede for someone. You can also write a prayer in which you praise the Lord for specific truths that you find in the passage that you are studying. And don't forget that you can praise and honor the Lord by sharing the truths that you found with someone else that day.

Because music has such a profound impact on us in so many ways, it is important to select music that lifts you up, and doesn't drag you down. It is much better to have a song in our minds about how God loves and leads us, rather than one about someone who rejected us, or who ran off with our lover! I have done extensive study on the power of music, so I understand its power to depress or to lift us up. Even the use of vibrato on an organ can make people sad! Be careful. Use music to help you, not hurt you.

Does God Always Answer Prayer?

We can be experiencing a well-balanced prayer life, using music to help us in our worship, and yet, still have the feeling that our prayers are not getting past the ceiling. We hear about prayers being answered, but we wonder if ours are.

I cannot tell you the number of people who have said to me that their prayers feel as though they are not getting past the ceiling. What do you think they are experiencing? Why do they, and maybe you, feel this way at times? Does God sometimes fail to answer our prayers? Is He the one keeping them from getting past the ceiling?

The Bible has much to say about prayer and answers to prayer. God's Word should always be the central focus when we seek to understand and practice effective prayer. (We will study the role of the Bible and prayer in the next chapter.) One verse that helps us to understand how best to answer the question about whether God always answers prayer is found in I John 5:14-15.

> *This is the confidence we have in approaching God: that if we ask anything **according to his will**, he hears us. And if we know that he hears us—whatever we ask—we know that we have what we asked of him.*

The first answer to the question about whether God answers prayer is obviously the truth that prayer must be "according to God's will." You may wonder how we can know for sure what God's will is, and therefore to pray that way to assure that our prayers will be answered. There are some basic ways to know what God's will is, and to be certain about it before we make a request to God:

(1) *The will of God, what God wants, is often stated very clearly in the Bible.* Our responsibility is to study the Bible conscientiously, and with the Holy Spirit's guidance, to learn how to discern what God's will is. Jesus said that the Spirit is our 'teacher,' among the other things that He does for us. He is within us to 'lead us into all truth.' Our job is to be available and teachable, and to be diligent students of the Bible.

(2) *We are to ask God what His will is, not simply to try to figure it out.* It is often easier to assume that we know what He wants, so we fail to ask Him. But He wants us to

ask and *seek,* and He promises that we will *find*, if we faithfully search. (Mt. 7:7-8)

(3) *We are to learn how to discern God's will, through prayer, through times of worship and by listening to the impressions that He places in our hearts.* This is best accomplished as we spend time with Him. Learning how to listen to the promptings of God are very important. And as we do this on a regular basis, we will become more skilled at recognizing when He is leading us, or telling us something.

(4) *We must learn how to use our reasoning to understand God's will.* We should become more skilled at finding truth through reason, logic and experience. But we also must allow God to speak to us at times that might seem to be totally unreasonable. Learning how to 'be still and hear His voice' is urgent.

How God Answers Prayer

It is natural for us to want God to always answer our prayers ... when, where and how we ask Him to do so. Thankfully, however, our loving Father knows the best ways to respond to us. Sometimes, our requests are fulfilled immediately. At other times, God does not provide what we have pleaded with Him to give to us, or to do for us. It is especially at these times that we need to remember that He knows what is best for us. *His thoughts are not our thoughts, and His ways are not our ways. His ways are higher than our ways, and His thoughts than our thoughts.* (Isa. 55:8-9) If we believe that He knows what is best for us, and knows best how to bring that to fruition, then we should find comfort in knowing that what appears to us to be 'unanswered prayer' may be a Divine 'No' or 'Wait.' Trusting God's timing is especially difficult for us humans. Do you recall the promise that God gave to Sarah and Abraham: that they would conceive and bear a son, even though they were both advanced in years, and past child-bearing age? They believed God, but they were not patient enough to wait on His timing. They tried to bring about God's will in their own way...and their descendants are still fighting!

Let's take a closer look at God's 'Yes,' 'No,' and 'Wait' answers:

When God's answer is 'Yes.'

> *For no matter how many promises God has made, they are "Yes" in Christ. And so through him the "Amen" is spoken by us to the glory of God. (2 Cor. 1:20)*

Look closer at this verse. When it comes to claiming God's promises, the answer will always be 'Yes.' The problem arises when we try to discern which promises that God has made are for us to claim. In this verse Paul writes that ALL of God's promises are ones that we can claim as ours, as long as we are 'in Christ.' Does that mean that all Christians are IN Christ? In one way, the answer is 'yes.' If we have invited Jesus into our hearts, and given our lives to His Lordship, then we are 'in Him' forever. But there is more. There is the daily walk of being 'in Him.' Note the truths in the following verses that shed some light on this topic:

> *"If you remain in me and my words remain in you, ask what you wish, and it will be given to you." (John 15:7)*

When we abide in the Lord, remain vitally connected to Him, He will answer our prayers. We will receive that for which we ask. Living IN HIM assures us that our requests will be answered with a 'yes' from the Lord. But how do we know what is permissible to ask?

> *"I tell you the truth, my Father will give you whatever you **ask in my name**. Ask and you will receive, and your joy will be complete." (John 16:24)*

Another question comes to mind here: What does it mean to pray **in Jesus' name**? How can I be sure that I am praying this way, since it is one of the keys to being sure that I receive 'yes' answers from God when I pray? Although there is much written on the concept of the Lordship or Christ, it will suffice for us to understand certain truths about praying 'in Jesus' name:'

1. Jesus is the one who gives us the right to even approach Him or the Father in prayer. We should always acknowledge that fact when we pray.

2. Anything asked of Him or the Father should be something that He says is permissible to ask. This is why it is important to know the Scripture, as well as to learn how to listen to Him personally speak to us.

3. What we pray must be something that will bring honor and glory to Jesus.

4. What we ask for must be according to His will. We should always pray "Not my will, but yours be done," even when claiming a Bible promise. Why? Because sometimes the request might be legitimate, but the timing is wrong. And, sometimes we misunderstand when a Bible promise is for us. It is always safest to pray that "His will be done," that "glory and honor will come to Him," "that the granting of a request be made only if it is best."

Jesus repeatedly said that we should ask, seek and knock...and keep at it until something happens. And his half-brother, James, someone who obviously heard Jesus speak on the subject many times, said *"You do not have, because you do not ask."* (James 4:2) But he also wrote a warning about asking: *"When you ask, you do not receive, because you ask with wrong motives, that you may spend what you get on your pleasures."* (James 4:3) Therein is a stark warning for us, and the reason that I have suggested that we should always ask "according to His will," and "for His glory." Those prayers help keep us on track, and will eliminate any self-seeking requests that we might make.

When God's answer is 'No.'

Don't you just hate asking someone to do something for you, and they refuse? You had your hopes up, or had a deep need for some help...and the request was denied. What were some of your reactions? Anger? Depression? Feelings of rejection? Disappointment? You have more than likely felt some or all of these feelings. And the same thing happens when we get a 'No' answer from God, especially when we feel that the request was legitimate, and our need was great. Naturally, all of us want God to always answer 'yes.' Why wouldn't we? But when He answers 'No,' or the heavens seem silent, we can have pretty strong negative reactions.

Did you ever stop to think about the fact that even Jesus experienced a 'No' to His prayer to His Father, during one of the most difficult times in His life? It is easy to think that Jesus always had His prayers answered with a 'yes.' But He did not. One of His desperate requests to His Father was NOT answered with a 'Yes.'

> *"My Father, if it is possible, may this cup be taken from me. Yet not as I will, but as you will." (Matt 26:39)*

Jesus' request was made during a time of extreme pain and sorrow. *"My soul is overwhelmed with sorrow to the point of death. Stay here and keep watch with me."* (Matt. 26:38) He repeated His request to the Father three times. But the answer was the same: 'No.' Note the last way that Jesus phrased the request: *"My Father, if it is not possible for this cup to be taken away unless I drink it, may your will be done."* Obviously, the Father said 'No' to His precious Son, because there 'was no other way' for OUR redemption to be carried out. God the Father said 'No' to His Son in order for the debt of OUR sins to be paid. The 'greater good' was accomplished. Our salvation was purchased.

Did having to say 'No' to His Son cause sorrow to the heart of the Father? Of course it did. But He knew the 'greater good.' He knew the real reason for the pain and suffering. And we should remember these truths when the Father says 'No' to us. Since He knows the 'greater good,' He knows when the timing is wrong, or the granting of a request that we make is not in our best interest or in the center of His will. Although we may not ever understand why we are told 'No,' we must hold onto our faith...and trust Him even when we do not understand.

Paul also received a 'No' answer to a prayer request...about a situation that was causing him great duress, and a problem that he felt was hindering his ministry for the Lord. *"Three times I pleaded with the Lord to take it (a messenger of Satan which was tormenting him) away from me." (2 Cor. 12:8)* What was God's answer? 'No.' The answer was 'No.' But, as He sometimes does, God gave the reasons for His answer...at least some of them: (1) To keep Paul from becoming conceited because of His experiences with the Lord, and (2) That God's power would be made perfect in Paul's weaknesses. (vs. 7, 9) God wanted to teach Paul that he would experience more of God's power and strength when he was not filled with his own. That is a lesson which we all need to learn! God knows when a 'Yes' answer would be harmful for us.

When God's answer is 'Wait.'

There were several people in the Bible who experienced a 'wait' answer from the Lord. Mary and Martha were two of them. Their brother, Lazarus, was ill...to the point of death. Under great distress, they sent for Jesus...requesting that He come to them in their time of need...and He delayed. He waited. Their request that He come was denied. He waited. He made them wait. Things became worse. Lazarus died. Mary and Martha suffered the pain of loss, of course, but I am sure that they also experienced disappointment, anger, disillusionment, doubt and feelings of rejection. Their friend Jesus had not come. They had seen Him heal others. But He did not come when they needed Him. Their grief over the death of their brother must have been compounded. It seemed as though Jesus had let them down.

We know how the story, ended, however. Jesus did an even greater miracle among them: He raised Lazarus from the dead. "There was the greater good." There is always a 'greater good' to God's answer of 'wait.' We really must hold tightly to that truth, even when we cannot see what He is doing, or understand why He is waiting. And even if we never understand, we must believe that God always knows what is best...what the 'greater good' is.

Sometimes it is extremely difficult to wait on God to fulfill the promise that we know He has given to us. Abraham and Sarah had that difficulty. God told them that they would have a son, even though they both were past child-bearing age. They believed God...but when the answer did not come in what they considered a timely manner, they decided to help bring about the results themselves. Waiting for God to answer the promises that we know He has made to us...is very tough. But we must ask for His grace to wait...or we will bring about a disaster, as did Abraham and Sarah. And what they did...the solution they contrived...still is causing trouble today. The offspring of Hagar (Ismael) are people who are still at war against the offspring of Sarah (Isaac)...Arabs and Israelis.

One of the last words of instruction that Jesus told His disciples, before He ascended to His Father, was to 'wait.' *"Do not leave Jerusalem, but wait for the gift that my Father promised, which you have heard me speak about. For John baptized with water, but in a few days you will be baptized with the Holy Spirit."* (Acts 1:4-5)

Waiting is hard. Whether it is waiting on God to lead, for Him to answer a prayer, or for Him to bring about what He has already assured us that He will do…waiting is hard. We must remember that His timing is perfect, His will is always best, His knowledge is complete, and His love is assured. Trusting in His power, wisdom and goodness will help us wait in faith for His 'yes,' 'no,' or 'wait' answers to our prayers.

PRAYING, OR PLAYING?

I bowed my head,
   I thought to pray.
Alas! My mind -
   It would not stay.

I cried, "O God!"
   And bowed my heart.
This time I thought,
   "I've done my part."

Silence was all
   That filled the air,
Again I realized
   No answer to prayer

I searched His Word
   And there did find
'Twas my whole attitude,
   Not just my mind.

I humbly sought Him
   On bended knee.
This time He answered.
   He'd heard my plea.

- Poem by Martha Fraser

Key 3:

Understand the Role of Scripture in Prayer

I can remember (as a new Christian) wishing that there was an envelope that would show up on my doorstep each morning that would give me specific instructions from God for the day. And I also wished that there was a way to know specifically what He wanted me to do with my life, choices about school, what to major in, what job to train for, etc. I knew that I loved Him, and wanted to serve Him. I was so grateful that He had rescued me from a life of depression and discouragement that had nearly caused me to take my own life. I was sincere. I was eager to follow Him and to do His will, whatever that looked like. I wanted to prove to Him how grateful I was, and I didn't want to make any decisions that would cause me to wander off the pathway of truth, or to bring harm to Him or His causes.

    I discovered, however, as I continued to grow in my relationship with Him, that sometimes it is really quite difficult to know what He wants, how He is leading, and whether we are even on the right path at all. Thankfully, the two women who began discipling me were faithful to teach me the importance of studying the Word of God. God left us written instructions, as well as the indwelling Holy Spirit, to help guide us. He wants to speak to us, to have fellowship with us, to guide us on the right pathway, and to use us in kingdom work. Although we are still living in the flesh (still possessing the Adamic nature that wants to run its own life and to be god), the Lord has provided for us all that we need to be successful in living life in His will. And, of course, His main desire is that we love Him, and walk with Him. That is why we were created!

Among the helpful and necessary provisions that God has given to us is the Bible. He has gone to great lengths to have it compiled and preserved. It is a major tool in helping us walk successfully with Him while we are still on this earth. Among its benefits are: (1) food for our spirits; (2) strength for all of our needs; (3) comfort when we hurt; (4) guidance for the journey; (5) instructions for how life works best; and (6) wisdom and information about prayer. It is filled with truth...information about the character and love of God. It is our source of doctrine, our lifeline to things spiritual. And among its treasures are the promises that God has made to His children. We must learn what those are, and how to claim them for ourselves. The promises are some of the major ways that God releases His blessings to us. They are like checks which we present to the 'bank of heaven.' God always keeps His promises. It is urgent that we know what to do to claim them for ourselves. Money in the bank will do us no good if we don't know how to access it. It is tragic when the promises of God are not believed and claimed. Could it be that we are actually cheating ourselves out of blessings that God wants to readily give to us?

Claiming God's Promises

The first question that probably comes to mind when we think about claiming God's promises is "Which ones can I claim, since they were originally made to people in Bible times?" The best answer, I think, is found in 2 Cor. 1:20.

For no matter how many promises God has made, they are "yes" in Christ. And so through him the "Amen" is spoken by us to the glory of God.

What does this verse teach us? When we belong to Jesus, all of the promises that God made to His people refer to us as well. For instance, Isaiah 41:10 is a promise that God gave to the children of Israel:

So do not fear, for I am with you; do not be dismayed, for I am your God. I will strengthen you and help you; I will uphold you with my righteous right hand.

Can I also claim that promise? Can I be assured that God will also strengthen me and uphold me when I need Him? And, if so, how do I "claim this promise for myself?'" It is helpful to read 2 Cor. 1:20 again for the answer. IF I am *in* Christ (a believer who has trusted Him as Lord and Savior), then I can be assured that this promise is also for me! I can ask Him about it: "God, is this promise for me to claim?" And 2 Cor. 1:20 tells us how God will answer, and what my reaction to His answer should be. The answer will be "Yes, the promise is for you, because you are my child." My reaction should be "Amen," or "So be it," or "I'll take that." Claiming God's promises is as simple as that. Someone has said that our attitude should be "God said it, I believe it, and that settles it." I would like to add this statement: "God promised it; I believe it; I take it."

Because it is so important to learn what promises God has made to His children, and how we can claim them when we need them, I have found that it is helpful to color code[4] them as I discover them. I can remember when I was challenged to begin my own color-coding of Scripture. I used a concordance to help me find verses on specific topics. I began with the words 'prayer,' and 'pray.' I then looked up verses that actually used the word 'promise' in them. Through the years, whenever I come upon a verse that is a promise, I color-code it. This approach to finding and coloring promises has been extremely helpful to me. It is essential that we know what the promises are before we can claim them!

Another important thing to remember is that there are differences in **conditional** and **absolute** promises. *Conditional* promises are ones that require us to do, or stop doing, certain things, before we can receive what God has promised. *Absolute* promises do not have conditions to them. I will give some examples to help you understand the difference between these two types of promises.

2 Chron. 7:14 is a well-known Bible promise. Read it and see whether you think it is an absolute or conditional promise.

> *If my people, who are called by my name, will humble themselves and pray and seek my face and turn from their wicked ways, then will*

---

[4] If you are interested in learning how to color code your own Bible, you can find a booklet that I wrote on amazon.com. Search for it by using the title Color Coding Your Bible. It is only 99 cents for a digital version. If you need a hard copy, contact us at lamplighters-ministries.org.

I hear from heaven and will forgive their sin and will heal their land.

This promise is obviously a *conditional* one. There are things that we must do before God will hear and answer certain prayers. We must develop the habit of searching for, and meeting the conditions of prayer promises, if we want God to answer them!

Try another one:

His divine power has given us everything we need for life and goodness through our knowledge of him who called us by his own glory and goodness. Through these he has given us his very great and precious promises, so that through them you may participate in the divine nature and escape the corruption in the world caused by evil desires. (2 Peter 1:3-4)

These verses clearly show the role that 'claiming promises' has. Verse three is an *absolute* promise: God HAS already given to us everything that we need for life and godliness. That is a stated fact whether or not we believe it or claim it. And verse four tells us how to access this power to live life: we do it by claiming promises! The power is there, but it does not benefit us if we do not claim the promise. To me, this verse is the clearest evidence that learning how to claim promises is the major way to benefit from the blessings that God has already made readily available. When we don't claim a promise, we cheat ourselves out of tremendous blessings. We need to discover what promises God has made, check to see if they have conditions, meet the conditions, and then claim them! And how do we do that? In prayer. ANY promise that God makes in the Bible can be claimed, when we meet the pre-requisites.[5] God invites us, by OUR faith, to prove HIS faithfulness.

PRAYING THE SCRIPTURES

Most of us have trouble at times knowing how to express our prayers to God. It is in times like these that the Bible can be especially helpful to us. We can use the words of the Bible itself to express our prayers to God. We can either pray the exact words of the Scripture, or paraphrase them into our own words. The main point is to use the Bible to help us express our prayers to God. I will give a few examples here to explain how to do this.

Using the words of the Bible itself:

(1) When you are feeling guilt over sin or disobedience:

> *Create in me a pure heart, O God, and renew a steadfast spirit within me. Do not cast me from your presence or take your Holy Spirit from me. Restore to me the joy of your salvation and grant me a willing spirit, to sustain me.* (Ps. 51:10-12)

(2) When you need guidance from the Lord:

> *Show me your ways, O Lord, teach me your paths; Guide me in your truth and teach me, for you are my God my Savior, and my hope is in you all day long.* (Ps. 25:4-5)

---

[5] See the Appendix for a list of Bible promises, and how you can claim them in prayer.

(3) When you want to praise the Lord:

> *Worthy is the Lamb, who was slain, to receive power and wealth and wisdom and strength and honor and glory and praise!* (Rev. 5:12)

(4) When you pray for others:

> *And this is my prayer: that your love may abound more and more in knowledge and depth of insight, so that you may be able to discern what it best and may be pure and blameless unto the day of Christ, filled with the fruit of righteousness that comes through Jesus Christ – to the glory and praise of God.*
> (Phil. 1:9-11)

These are just a few of the many Scriptures that you can use to help you express your prayers to God. As an example of how to rephrase the verses in your own words, I will take the same verses and give you an example of how you could pray:

(1) Ps 51:10-11

> *Lord, I have sinned and need your cleansing. Please do not give up on me. I need for you to restore me back to fellowship with you. I want to walk with you and enjoy our time together, like I used to do before I sinned. Work in my heart to renew my spirit once again.*

(2) Ps. 25:4-5

> *Lord, I have lost my way. I do not know how to get back on the path. I am confused about what your will is for my life right now. But I know that you are my Lord. I know that I can trust you. I ask for your guidance in my life.*

(3) Rev. 5:12

> *O Lord, you are worthy of all of my praise. Your glory is wonderful. You died for us sinners. You deserve all honor and praise. I love you and desire to serve you forever.*

(4) Phil. 1:9-11

> *Lord, I ask that you help my friends come to love you even more than they now do. Please fill their minds and hearts with the knowledge of how wonderful you are, so that they will understand the best way to live, and that they will grow in their walk of holiness. Help them to be so filled with righteousness that it will bring much honor and glory to you.*

I recommend that you include times when you actually pray the Scriptures as they are recorded, but it is also a good practice to use your own words to express the same truths. By doing these types of prayers, you will grow in your ability to share with Him the deep love and devotion that is in your heart.

The Bible Helps Us Know What to Pray

"Is it OK to pray about everything?" the new Christian asked the pastor. "Some of what I pray about seems so small to bother God with?"

Do you have the same question about prayer? Do you wonder if you should pray about what seems too trivial to bring before Almighty God, the King of the Universe? Doesn't He want me to handle what I can handle, and only bring to Him major problems or questions? How can I know what is OK to spend time praying about?

Before we begin to look at these and other questions, we need to be sure of one thing: God is our loving heavenly Father. Nothing is too small or trivial for us to talk with Him about. But, it is possible that we are wasting our time praying about things that He has already addressed in the Bible. Are there answers to some of our questions that are already recorded in God's Word? Wouldn't it be amazing if God's children offered prayer requests that He always answered affirmatively...that He said 'Yes' to everything we requested, when the prayers were in accordance with His will and purpose? Is there a way for that to happen? What would we have to understand before we offered such prayers? The best place to find the answers for these questions is in the Bible, or course.

The Bible gives clear guidelines about what God has said that His children should be bringing to Him in prayer. Consider the following verses and instructions:

1. We can pray for help and strength if we are afflicted, ill-treated, or suffering evil.

> *Is anyone among you in trouble? Let them pray. Is anyone happy? Let them sing songs of praise. (James 5:13)*

This type of prayer is easy for most of us. And even non-believers will usually reach out to God in prayer when they are suffering in some way. We pray when we are in trouble, but sometimes we forget to do what James also says in this verse: To sing songs of praise when we are happy.

I have two little pups that live in my home. They teach me much about God. The smaller one, a male Shih Tzu that only weighs about 10 lbs., often comes to me for comfort when he hurts himself. His older and heavier companion sometimes hurts him when they play with each other. Also, he seems to find more things in the yard to step on. He is also timid around people unless he knows them, so he often runs to me out of fear. I try to comfort him, or heal his hurts. But I also enjoy times when he simply wants to sit on my lap or beside me. If he wanted nothing to do with me except when he needed comfort, I would feel cheated. I am certain that God must feel the same way about us at times.

2. We are encouraged to pray for the sick.

> *Is anyone among you sick? Let them call the elders of the church to pray over them and anoint them with oil in the name of the Lord. And the prayer offered in faith will make the sick person well; the Lord will raise them up. If they have sinned, they will be forgiven. (James 5:14-15)*

The main truth to get from these verses is that people on praying ground have great power when it comes to healing the sick. But I believe that there is a major misunderstanding about the meaning of the phrase: 'the prayer offered in faith.' Faith IS NOT simply believing hard enough that someone is going to be healed, that God is obligated to heal them. The faith of some has been harmed, when they believed strongly that the person for whom they prayed would be healed, and they were not. The person who offered the prayer can sometimes feel guilty...believing that they failed the person and God by not having enough faith when they prayed.

The best way to understand what this verse is trying to teach us, (other than that we should pray for the sick), can best be understood by examining the definition of the word 'faith.' The biblical definition of faith is: "the leaning of the entire personality on God, in absolute trust and confidence in His power, wisdom and goodness." It is trusting God. It is believing that God has all power and wisdom, and that He is a good God...always. We can always depend on God to do what He wants to do, and we believe that He always knows what is best, even when we do not understand it.

The 'prayer of faith' is to believe what God has told us is His will regarding the healing of a sick person. Sometimes it is His will to heal them, and sometimes it is not. The 'prayer of faith' is a prayer voiced when God tells us what His will is for the sick person, and we claim the healing that God said was His will for them. I think that this is why the people, whom we summon to the bedside of someone who is ill, should be 'elders.' Elders are those spiritual leaders who have walked with God by faith for many years, and who know how to hear what the will of God is regarding a person or situation. When they do not hear a clear word from God, they are able to pray and leave the person or situation in His hands.

The anointing of oil can mean a couple of things: Anointing oil was historically associated with the work of God, and most especially the Spirit of God. In the days when this epistle was written, oil was often used to help heal people, to bring down their fever, etc. I believe that this passage is a good reminder that we should always join medical intervention with prayer, in order to bring about the healing of those whom God wills to be healed. Our job is to be faithful to God's Spirit, and to pray and listen for what the will of God is for those who are sick. If we do not know what God's will is regarding a person's healing, we pray anyway. We continue to pray for the person, asking that God's will be done, and that He will fill their hearts with His grace and peace. We can be certain that this prayer is always His will!

3. We are told to pray for each other, if we have fallen into sin. In this same passage in James, we are instructed to pray about spiritual illness as well. We all need to be 'restored to a spiritual tone of mind and heart. (James 5:16, Amp. N.T.) This happens when we "*confess our sins to each other and pray for each other.*" Unfortunately, it is not easy to do this! But when we realize the harm that can come to us from unconfessed sin, it should be easier to admit our failures! Of course, we do not arbitrarily go around telling everyone about all of our sins. We should only trust those people who are spiritually mature, and who are walking with the Lord themselves. True accountability partners are necessary for our spiritual growth.

4. We can pray about the weather if it is concerning God's glory.

Elijah was a human being, even as we are. He prayed earnestly that it would not rain, and it did not rain on the land for three and a half years. Again he prayed, and the heavens gave rain, and the earth produced its crops. (James 5:17-18)

There are quite a few prayers that are prayed about the weather: "Pray that it won't rain on my birthday party." "Pray that it will be cooler tomorrow, because I am going to be working outside." I have always been amused at what 'weather-conversations' one of my friends and I have. She wants it to snow in the winter, and I do not. She wants it to be cold, and I do not. I am sure that we cancel each other out on most weather-related prayers!

I think that James is not saying it is OK to pray for it not to rain on my outdoor picnic, although God loves for us to talk with Him about everything that is on our minds. I think that James is reminding us that such weather-related prayers should involve God's glory and the true welfare of His children. So, when we gather to pray for rain on a parched land, we should take our umbrella to the prayer meeting! And when someone is facing an impending storm or earthquake, or who is scheduled to travel in inclement weather, of course, we should pray about it.

5. We should be praying for those who do not know Jesus as Savior. One of the roles of the Holy Spirit is to convict people of their need of Jesus. We can ask the Spirit to convict people, and to cause them to realize their need of

Jesus. As you pray, remember that you are not trying to convince the Spirit to deal with a non-Christian. He already desires to do that. What you are doing is being a 'channel of power' through whom the Spirit can work to convict someone. I find that an illustration about our being an extension cord can help us understand our role in the Spirit's work. When we pray, we are 'plugging into God, the ultimate power source,' in order that the needed power of conviction can be released through us to the lost person. We ask the Spirit to draw a lost person to Jesus, and to convict them of their need to be saved.

When he comes, he will prove the world to be in the wrong about sin and righteousness and judgment: about sin, because people do not believe in me; about righteousness, because I am going to the Father, where you can see me no longer; and about judgment, because the prince of this world now stands condemned. (John 16: 8-10)

6. We should pray that Christians will have an opportunity, and boldness, to witness about Jesus. Paul asked the Ephesian believers to pray that his spoken words would clearly and fearlessly make known the mystery of the gospel. We are not asking God to do something that He does not already want to be done! We again are simply pipelines through whom the power of God can flow, as we go to the throne of God and pray; and God does the work! We are aiming the water hose where the water is needed.

> *"Pray also for me that when I open my mouth, words may be given me so that I will fearlessly make known the mystery of the gospel, for which I am an ambassador in chains. Pray that I may declare it fearlessly as I should."* (Eph. 6:19)

7. We are told to pray for people in authority over us. We may not agree with leaders who are over us…those in government, at our workplace, or even in our church. But God said to pray. They need power to do what they are attempting to do. We are not trying to tell God to make them do what we want them to do; we are sending prayer-power so that they will hear from God, and will have His empowerment to accomplish His will. Many leaders remain weak, selfish or ignorant about how best to serve…because we are failing to send them the power that they need to do their jobs! And when they are not following the will of God, we should pray for the Spirit to convict them of this.

> *I urge, first of all, that requests, prayers, intercession and thanksgiving be made for everyone – for kings and all those in authority, that we may live peaceful and quiet lives in all godliness and holiness.* (I Timothy 2:1-2)

8. Jesus told us to pray for our enemies, for those who persecute and mistreat us. It is important to take notice of some other instructions that Jesus gave, in this context of His teaching, about praying for those who mistreat us.

> *"But I tell you who hear me: love your enemies, do good to those who hate you, bless those who curse you, pray for those who mistreat you. If someone strikes you on one cheek, turn to him the other also. If someone takes your cloak, do not stop him from taking your cloak. Give to everyone who asks you, and if anyone takes what belongs to you, do not demand it back. Love your enemies, do good to them, and lend to them without expecting to get anything back."*
> (Luke 6:27-30, 35)

This seems to be an impossible assignment! It is so unnatural for us to do this, to forgive others and to treat well those who have mistreated us! But, in the midst of what seems so impossible is a key message for us: "pray for those…" When we connect to the source of power through prayer, our lives will be changed, our attitudes adjusted, and God's love and forgiveness can actually flow into us, and then through us to others. We have cut off our own healing and empowerment by failing to pray for our enemies.

9. We are instructed to pray for our material needs (daily bread). One of the biggest obstacles to overcome is the way we look at prayer. Because we sometimes have to 'ask other humans' for things, and even at times have to beg and plead with them, we think we have to do the same thing with God. What we forget is the fact that our Father loves to shower blessings on us. He is the great Giver, the great Blesser. He is the owner of the Universe, the one who owns the 'bank of heaven.' He tells us to come to get what we need, when we need it. We can come to get whatever we need, even daily provisions. If we ask wrongly, or when we want things that are not His will for us, He will help us to see that. He also helps us understand that when He refuses to give us something, THAT is also a blessing.

> *"If you then, though you are evil, know how to give good gifts to your children, how much more will your Father in heaven give the Holy Spirit to those who ask Him."* (Luke 11:13)

James tells us that there are other reasons for why we are not receiving the blessings which we seek. *"You do not have, because you do not ask. When you do ask, you do not receive, because you ask with wrong motives, that you may spend what you get on your pleasures."* (James 4:2-3) Either we do not pray at all, or we pray wrongly. We must learn these simple, yet profound, truths about prayer...and just how easy it is for our own hearts to deceive us!

10. We need to pray for the spiritual well-being of fellow believers in Jesus. We all need God's wisdom in order to understand how to navigate life as it should be lived. We all are weak, and need God's empowerment. We all struggle with the old nature, the self that continues to lead us away from God, instead of toward Him. We all want to play 'king of the hill,' taking charge of our own lives, instead of allowing Jesus to be Lord.

What can help us in this internal struggle? Most helpful are the prayers of fellow believers. Paul includes many of his prayers for fellow believers, in the letters that he wrote to them. It would do us well to study them closely, and to make it a practice to pray these prayers for one another.

> *I keep asking that the God of our Lord Jesus Christ, the glorious Father, may give you the Spirit of wisdom and revelation, so that you may know him better. I pray that the eyes of your heart may be enlightened in order that you may know the hope to which he has called you, the riches of his glorious inheritance in the saints, and his incomparably great power for us who believe. That power is like the working of his mighty strength, which he exerted in Christ when he raised him from the dead and seated him at the right hand in the heavenly realms..."*
> (Eph. 1:20)

Can you even imagine the difference in our lives and in our churches if we would regularly pray this prayer for each other? The potential empowerment is beyond our ability to even comprehend. We settle for weakness, when God's power is available.

11. We can pray for someone's deliverance.

> *So Peter was kept in prison, but the church was earnestly praying to God for him.*
> (Acts 12:5)

In this passage, the church had gathered to pray for Peter's release from prison. The amusing thing about this account was the church's shock when God answered their prayers! Were they not expecting God to respond to their requests, or were they just surprised that He did so very quickly, or in a way that they did not expect? We do not know the answer to those questions, but we DO know that it is right for us to pray for people who are in any kind of 'prison.' Many Christians are in bondage in various kinds of prisons: addictions, unhealthy relationships, traumatic childhood events, or spiritual ignorance and incorrect theology. Whatever the prison is that keeps people in bondage, we need to help set them free through prayer.

12. We should pray for the Lord's return.

> *He who testifies to these things says, "Yes, I am coming soon." Amen. Come quickly, Lord Jesus.* (Rev. 22:20)

I believe that most Christians know that Jesus is coming back one day. There are many different opinions about what that will look like, what will be going on when it happens, etc. But I am not sure that many of us are praying and asking for Him to come on back NOW! I remember discussing the topic in a Bible class at the university where I taught. One student responded, when I asked if they were looking forward to the Lord's return. She said, "Yes, I am glad, but I want Him to wait awhile. I have a lot of things that I want to do first." Another student said, "I want to at least graduate from college first." What is your reply to the same question?

13. **We should ask the Lord to keep us from falling into temptation.**

   "Watch and pray so that you will not fall into temptation. The spirit is willing, but the body is weak." (Mt. 26:20)

Unfortunately, it is easy to think that we are strong enough to reject temptations that come our way. But we are not. In fact, we often don't even realize that we are being tempted, until we have succumbed! If Jesus thinks that we need to use prayer as a way to avoid temptation, then it is obvious that we need to do what He said! We may be willing to stay pure, but our flesh is very weak.

14. **We must pray that the Lord protect us from the evil one.** This is mentioned by Jesus in the model prayer that He taught His disciples (Mt. 6:13). Not only did He say that we must ask the Lord to keep us from temptation, we are to pray that we be delivered from the evil one himself. In Jesus' prayer that is recorded in John 17, the Savior prayed earnestly that the Father 'protect us from the evil one.' I wonder how many of us realize just how important this prayer is. We should pray it daily for ourselves and for others.

15. **We should ask the Lord to send laborers into His harvest field** (Mt. 9:38). I used to wonder about the meaning of this prayer until I read it in the Amplified version. I wondered why we should be asking the Lord to send out laborers into the harvest fields, when it is obvious that it is His will that we evangelize our world. Here is how the

Amplified version of the Bible translates this verse: *"So pray to the Lord of the harvest to **force out and thrust out** laborers into His harvest."* Jesus is saying that we must pray for God's power to 'make people go out, to push them and persuade them to go into the harvest field.' When the power of God comes on a person's life, he/she is more likely to answer the call of God to go work in the harvest fields, and to go wherever God leads.

When I began to understand that God has chosen to let us be a 'channel' or 'conduit' through whom He works in the world, this verse makes more sense. This 'free translation' of the verse (another way of understanding what Jesus is attempting to convey), might help you understand what I am trying to say: "Connect up to me, plug into me, the Power Source, and send the power to believers as a way to persuade them to do what is My will: to evangelize the world." We are not trying to convince the Lord at all. We are being an 'extension cord' through whom He can work to persuade and empower laborers. And, as we pray, our own hearts will be convicted to answer the call!

16. We should pray for protection from evil doers.

> *Deliver me from my enemies, O God; protect me from those who rise up against me. Deliver me from evildoers and save me from bloodthirsty men.* (Ps. 59:1-2)

You don't have to read many psalms, especially the ones written by David, to see that praying for protection and deliverance from one's enemies was a prevalent theme. It was not until I had an experience of actually having my life threatened by someone, that I realized how urgent it is to pray this prayer. Many Christians, in different countries of the world, pray this prayer earnestly every day. Some are even losing their lives because of their faith. If we do not have a need to pray this prayer for ourselves, we most certainly should pray it for those who do need it.

17. We can pray when we are anxious about anything.

> *Do not be anxious about anything, but in everything, by prayer and petition, with thanksgiving, present your requests to God.*
> (Phil 4:6)

Since anxiety is something that we all face, we should study this passage in detail. There are instructions about how to pray when we are worried or upset, a common condition which we all face. Note first, that we are NOT to be anxious about anything. Consequently, we need to 'run to the Lord in prayer' when we do experience anxiety of any kind. Too often, we accept worry as a natural part of life. The Bible clearly tells us *not* to accept it, but to go to the Lord in prayer about it.

And Paul also tells us HOW to pray: with *prayer* (supplication: the 'Oh, help!' prayer that we lift to the Father when we don't know what to ask); *petition*: when we do know specific things to ask the Father; and then to wrap up all of the prayers with *thanksgiving*, a prayer that affirms that we believe that God is going to handle everything that is causing us anxiety. The result will be a peace that we cannot understand...one that guards our hearts and minds. Anxiety should always be a catalyst that pushes us into prayer.

18. We need to be praying for all Christians.

And pray in the Spirit on all occasions with all kinds of prayers and requests. With this in mind, be alert and always keep on praying for all the saints. (Eph. 6:18)

I was recently studying about prayer with a friend. We were examining verses that give instructions about how to pray. We came upon this one in Ephesians 6. The last phrase caught my attention, and convicted me. It is easy for me to pray for my friends and family, my fellow church members, and for those who request prayer. But Paul is telling us that we must keep on praying *for all the saints*: Christians all over the world. Our fellow believers in other countries especially need our prayers to help them face their daily challenges. It is a joy to know that there are no geographical or time barriers to prayer! The only problem is our failure to do it.

Look back over the prayers in this section. Are there areas that you are neglecting, or perhaps you have never included in your prayers? The Bible is filled with prayers and instructions about how to pray correctly. We can never know all that there is to know about the wonderful mystery of prayer. Have you ever wondered why God wants to actually involve us in His wonderful work in the world? There are many questions about prayer that will take us a lifetime to explore, and to even begin to understand. I do not even pretend to know, nor am I attempting to share, all that there is to understand about the wonderful privilege of prayer. But I hope that this book will at least encourage you in your personal search to know more about prayer, and to actually spend time walking and talking with Your Lord.

What is permissible to ask God for, or request that He do for us? Jesus told us to "ask and we would receive." But sometimes we wonder what is permissible to ask. Here is a list of good places to **start** in our 'prayer of asking.' Spend the rest of your life adding to the list!

1. For forgiveness: (Mt 6:12)
2. For daily necessities: (Mt 6:11: 6:33)
3. For good gifts from God: (Mt 7:11)
4. For the presence and power of the Holy Spirit: (Luke 11:13)
5. For mercy: (Ps 6:9; 86:6-7)
6. For strength: (Ps 86:16; 29:11)
7. For peace: (Ps 29:11; John 14:27)
8. For the Spirit to teach us: (John 14:26)
9. For the Spirit to help us pray: (Rom 8:26)
10. For rest: (Mt 11:28-30)
11. For the "river" to flow within us: (John 7:38-39)
12. Where the good path is: (Jer.6:16)
13. For rain: (Zech.10:1)
14. For wisdom to understand our trials: (James 1:5)

We must be careful to learn the difference between asking for something, and claiming or 'faith-ing' (believing and accepting by faith) something that God has already promised. Most of our 'asking' should probably be 'faith-ing' and receiving...and thanking. And don't forget Eph. 3:20: *"He is able to do immeasurably more than all we ask or imagine...."*

What are Some Things that People in the Bible Prayed About?

It is always a good thing to study the lives of people in the Bible, to learn from their experiences...what they did right, and what mistakes they made. I have compiled a list of a few requests that people made to God, or intercessions that they made for others. I suggest that you go to each of the passages to learn more of the specifics that can guide your own prayers.

1. To recover from illness. (2 Kings 8:8-9)

2. For wisdom and knowledge to lead. (2 Chron. 1:7-103)

3. For safe travel. (Ezra 8:21)

4. To always dwell in God's presence. (Ps 27:4)

5. Keep falsehood far away, to give neither poverty nor riches, only daily bread. (Prov. 30:8)

6. For someone's salvation. (Rom 10:1)

7. Not to hold someone's sin against them. (Acts 6:60)

8. That others have a spirit of wisdom and power. (Eph. 1:18-19)

9. That others might have the revelation to know Jesus better. (Eph. 1:17)

10. That others be strengthened and learn the fullness of

God's love. (Eph. 3:16-19)

11. That others may be filled with the fruit of righteousness and be able to discern the best. (Phil 1:9-11)

12. That God might open doors for the gospel to be proclaimed. (Col 4:3)

What prayers from this list have been missing in your own prayer life? Are you willing to add these things to your prayers?

What Should We Never Pray?

We have spent most of the time in this chapter addressing the topic of what we *should* be praying to the Lord about. But are there things that we should NOT pray about or ask God for? This is not a question about whether something is too trivial to bring to the Lord. It is a question about whether there are things that the Bible clearly tells us *not* to include in our prayers. Consider the following:

1. We must never ask for anything that we know is contrary to the will of God. There are many times when we do not know what God's will is. In such times as those, we should ask the Lord NOT to hear or answer anything that is not in His will. But when we DO know what the Bible teaches, that something IS NOT His will, it is wrong to ask the Lord for it. Psalm 106 gives us a stern example of what might happen when we insist on doing our own will over God's will.

> *"But, they soon forgot what he had done and did not wait for his counsel. In the desert, they gave*

in to their craving; in the wasteland they put God to the test. So he gave them what they asked for, but sent a wasting disease upon them."

Jeremiah 4:11 helps us understand more about this principle: *"Do not pray for the welfare of this people,"* because that prayer would have been in conflict with what God had already revealed about His people, and the resulting punishment for their sin and willful disobedience.

2. We must not ask God for whatever comes from our own sinful lusts. James wrote, *"You ask and do not receive, because you ask with wrong motives, so that you may spend it on your pleasures."* (James 4:3) Because we know that God wants to bless His children, sometimes we think that we can ask for worldly wealth or other 'things' that we want to own. Many Christians get caught up in the frenzy to obtain wealth, fancy clothes, new cars and clothes. In themselves, there is nothing wrong with 'things.' But when they lure us away from maintaining a close relationship with our heavenly Father, they are definitely wrong. The Spirit can help us keep alert for the subtle ways that our flesh draws us away from God. It is even easy for religious activity, or the desire for a prestigious ministry position, to become a lure that leads us into praying for the wrong things!

3. We must never pray when our heart is filled with doubt, unless we are asking God to help us with that doubt! James reminds us that we are to 'ask in faith without doubting.' (James 1:6-8) We must never be double-minded when we pray, wanting both God's will and ours. It is easy for us to try to change God's mind, hoping that He will agree with what we want! If we do not believe that God has the power or desire to do something, then it is useless to pray for it.

4. We should never ask God to do what He has told US to do. We must always do what we are able to do; then we can pray for God to provide what is beyond our control. Prayer is not a substitute for work. But Jesus said that without Him, we can do nothing. (John 15: 5) How do we maintain a healthy balance between doing something by ourselves, and asking God to do it? Paul received helpful instruction from Jesus when he asked the Lord to remove a 'thorn in his flesh.' Jesus told him that His power would be stronger when Paul recognized his weakness, and thereby was forced to rely on Jesus' strength. (2 Cor. 12:10)

Let me try to make this clearer by citing a recent experience that I had. I was asked to lead a series of Bible studies at a local church. My responsibility was to study and prepare. I enlisted the prayer support of others. I had prepared, and was quite capable of presenting the information. I have been a Bible teacher for many years, and earned a PhD. I received the Teacher of the Year Award at the university where I was teaching. I have had years of experience teaching, and am qualified academically to teach the material. Why did I ask for prayer, some might wonder? I asked for prayer because I cannot ever do what only God can do: speak to the hearts of people, and change them spiritually. I do not ask that He do what I am capable of and responsible for doing. I do my part. But I pray earnestly, and ask others to pray. I want Him to use me as a vessel through whom He will speak to hearts and transform lives!

5. We must never ask God to overlook our sin and disobedience. You may wonder if people ever do this...ask God to overlook their sin. Unfortunately, we sometimes do that without realizing it. When we make excuses for why we do not change, or why we do not do what we know is God's will, are we not actually asking, or at least expecting, God to overlook our sin? We excuse. We rationalize. We postpone. We are really asking that God understand, and not hold us accountable for our disobedience.

6. We should not ask that the Lord save someone. Let me clarify this statement, before you scratch me off of your list, as being a liberal heretic! We ARE to pray for the salvation of people. Paul was earnest in his desire and prayer that Israelites come to know God (Romans 10:1). God definitely wants everyone to be saved (I Tim. 2:4). Jesus died for the entire world. We are to pray for His laborers. We are to share God's truth with non-believers. But nowhere are we taught to ask God to save someone. We should ask that He CONVINCE them of their need of Him, to send someone to tell them the truth, to use us to share with them, etc. God is more than willing to save them when they believe in and accept His Son. We can plead with God to continue to work on the hearts of a nonbeliever, but to ask Him to save someone is really asking Him to coerce or make them do something that the person is resisting. God never overrides a person's free choice. But He can lovingly draw them and heavily convict them, when we pray.

I hope you understand the points I have been trying to make. We absolutely must pray for the unsaved. But it is urgent for us to pray in the correct way. It is a privilege to pray for those who do not know Jesus. But we must do it correctly, for it to be effective. And we must be living in obedience to Him ourselves, in order for our prayers to be powerful.

God's Word is our guide for prayer and for life. We must be diligent students of it, if we want to understand and grow in our life of prayer. The Bible is God's sword against Satan's deceit, attacks, and temptations. Jesus quoted it three times when He faced those 40 days of temptation in the wilderness. We must know how to use God's Word against our enemy, and to let it be the guide for our prayers. Never underestimate the prominence that the Bible must hold in your life, if you want your prayers to be powerful and your relationship with God to be enjoyable and productive.

Key 4:

Study Jesus' Prayer Life and Instructions

Jesus not only taught us the importance of prayer, He demonstrated it in His own life. He often slipped away from the crowd and His disciples to spend time with His Father. He also prayed on many other occasions, and people heard Him talk with God. He was, and is, the Master Teacher. He is the ultimate role model for us regarding prayer. In our quest to grow in our practice of prayer, it is essential that we study the life of Jesus, what He said, and what He did. We will look first at how, when, and what He prayed, and then we will study what He taught about prayer.

The Prayer Life of Jesus

Jesus modeled prayer. He spent time with His Father. He prayed alone, and He prayed in public. We can learn much about prayer by simply observing His relationship with the heavenly Father. He prayed often; He drew aside to be with His Father. So must we. He sought His Father's guidance and will. So must we. He interceded for those who were dear to Him. So must we. It will be helpful for you to read the following accounts of His life of prayer, and to make notes on what you need to remember to practice in your own life.

1. *Jesus prayed before selecting His disciples.* (Lk. 6: 41-2) We must remember to ask the Father for direction concerning decisions that we must make.

2. *He prayed at His baptism.* (Luke 3:21-22) We should pray when we are following the Lord in any act of obedience.

3. *He prayed before He did the miracle of the feeding of the 5,000 and the 4,000.* (Jn. 6:11; Mt. 14:19; Mk. 6:41; Luke 9:16) Whenever we are working to accomplish God's purposes, we should pray.

4. *Jesus prayed before He raised Lazarus from the dead.* (Jn. 11:41-42) Although we will more than likely never perform a miracle like this one, there are miraculous things that God wants to accomplish through each one of us. We need to pray, and submit to whatever He wants us to do in kingdom work. It is important to remember that when a soul comes to know Jesus as Savior, the new birth is a wonderful miracle! Perhaps if we prayed more, we would see this happen more when we minister and witness to others.

5. *When Jesus prayed, the appearance of His face changed, and His clothing became as bright as a flash of lightning.* (Luke 9:28-29) It is important to realize that prayer transforms us! It is impossible to spend time in the Father's presence without positive results. That is not WHY we pray, but it is a wonderful benefit.

6. *Jesus prayed when the disciples returned from a mission trip on which He had sent them.* (Luke 10:21) The disciples were ecstatic over the things that had happened when they went on mission. Jesus, however, told them to be careful to

rejoice over the right things. He reminded them that the greatest joy is remembering that their names are written in heaven…that they belong to God. Jesus then began praising His Father. It will do us well to remember to praise God for anything and everything that He is able to accomplish through our service to others.

7. *He laid His hands on and blessed little children.* (Mk. 10: 13-16) The Amplified Version of these versions indicate that Jesus 'fervently invoked a blessing' on the little children. We need to be people who will fervently bless people through our prayers for them.

8. *Jesus shared His heart with His Father.* When He was feeling troubled over what He was about to face, He submitted everything to the Father's will. He also told the Father that He knew it was His time to be crucified. He asked the Father to glorify His own name through what Jesus was about to experience. (John 12:27) It is so important for us to share how we feel with the Lord, and to submit to His will as we ask for His grace. We should also pray for Him to bring glory to Himself from everything we experience, whether it is good or painful.

9. *During the Passover meal with His disciples, Jesus prayed a blessing on the food and drink, as He did when He multiplied the loaves and fish to feed the crowds.* (Mt. 26:26) He did the same thing after His resurrection, when he met at the home of the Emmaus disciples. (Lk. 24:30) We should always express our gratitude to God for our food, as well as give Him thanks for other blessings.

10. *He prayed for Peter, that his faith not fail.* (Lk. 22:31) This is certainly something that we should pray for ourselves and for others.

11. *He blessed the disciples before His ascension into heaven.* (Lk. 24:50) How wonderful it will be if we remember to do this, whenever we have the opportunity…to bless our loved-ones, before we leave to go to heaven.

There are many more accounts in the Bible of Jesus praying: alone, on the mountain, all night long, in the Garden of Gethsemane, on the cross, etc. He was a person of prayer. And, how wonderful to know that Jesus hasn't stopped praying, just because He went to heaven. He is still interceding on our behalf! (Heb. 7:25; Rom. 8:34; I Jn. 2:1) Let's praise Him for His daily prayers for us, for His walk with His Father when He was here on earth, and for His willingness to go to the cross to redeem us.

Some of the Things that Jesus Taught us About Prayer

Jesus wants us to know the joy of walking with Him. He wants us to experience the power and transformation that result from a close walk with Him. He wants us to be channels through which He can bless and draw others to Himself. He wants us to know about and to experience just how wonderful it is to walk in communion with God. So, He taught about prayer, and preserved those instructions for us to have. Let's look at some of the important things that He taught about prayer.

One day, when the disciples observed their 'Rabbi' praying, they asked Him to teach them how to pray. Before He gave them the prayer that we now call the 'Lord's Prayer' or the 'Model Prayer,' He taught them some important things that we need to learn and practice.

He first taught them that it was important NOT to pray like the hypocrites did. Those 'play-actors' liked to pray standing in the synagogues and on the street corners, in order to be seen and applauded by others. (Mt. 6:5-6) There is really nothing quite as disgusting to us, and to God, as those who use false spirituality to try to impress others. Jesus said not to do that. He said that secret prayer is more important than praying to impress other people. When we pray, we should not try to look good in the eyes of others. We need to share our heart with God.

Another thing that Jesus taught them was that they should not babble repeatedly about things. We won't be heard simply because we keep repeating a request! It is erroneous to think that we can talk God into doing something, simply by attempting to wear Him down with our repeated prayers. This is one reason that we need to do a careful study of Jesus' teachings about prayer. It is easy for us to be doing it all wrong!

Jesus then taught the disciples 'how they should pray.' (Mt. 6:9) The emphasis was on HOW...not that they should always, and only, pray certain words and phrases. Let's take a look at what the Model prayer is, and what lessons and principles Jesus was communicating to them...and to us.

The Model Prayer

The Model prayer in Mt. 6:9-14 helps us to understand the *elements* that should be included in prayer.

1. We should be sure to begin our times of prayer and fellowship with God with praise and worship. Praise is the normal result of a true focus on the One to whom we are praying, and with whom we are fellowshipping. He is our Father; He is in heaven, the place of authority and glory. He is the King of Kings in all of His majesty. And, most importantly, He is our Father.

2. We should always seek, and to pray, that the Father's will be done on earth as it is in heaven. This kind of prayer will help to keep us focused on what is really important, rather than on the fleeting desires that we humans tend to have. His will should be supreme...the most important thing that we desire...even when we do not know exactly what that is.

3. We should ask for our daily needs. Jesus reminds us that the Father loves to provide for His children. Just as He provides for the birds of the air and the flowers of the field, He promises to provide whatever we need. The reason that we present our requests to the Lord is not to persuade Him to provide for us. It is the way that we receive what we need. This kind of prayer acknowledges His care for us, and it stimulates our faith to trust Him for every need, big and small.

4. Asking the Lord to forgive us for our sins is another important request that we should make each day. But we should also stop to think about what those sins are! When we do realize just how much we sin, it can make us more conscientious about avoiding the temptations that led us to commit sin in the first place. Also, we must remember that we are obligated to forgive others. Failure to do so blocks

God's forgiveness of us. Jesus knew that we would have a tendency to forget the importance of extending forgiveness to others, so he repeated that truth immediately following the model prayer. That is the only one of the teachings in the model prayer about which He elaborated. This shows us its importance...if we want to pray effectively. Sins must be cleansed and forgiven, and forgiveness must be extended to those who have sinned against us.

5. We need to pray about temptation. Why would Jesus teach them to ask God *'not to lead them into temptation?'* He Himself was *'led by the Spirit into the desert to be tempted by the devil.'* (Matt. 4: 1) We can only guess why He taught them to make this request to God, but it is clear that He taught them to pray to the Father *'to be delivered from evil (the Evil one).'* Perhaps Jesus was helping the disciples understand their own propensity to temptation...that it was something that they needed help with in order to stay away from sin of any kind. We are certainly more likely to follow Jesus when we are delivered from both temptation and the devil. Also, when we pray these things, it helps us be more alert to the entrapments of sin that are everywhere.

6. *'For Yours is the kingdom and the power and the glory'* is always a great way to end a time of prayer. We need to constantly recognize that what really matters in life is His power and glory. We are to be busy doing kingdom-things. We are to pray for things that matter in eternity. We are not to ask God to do things that hurt kingdom people or kingdom activities. It is necessary to be reminded that we are not in control, He is!

Although Jesus gave the Model Prayer as a model, not just a prayer to say, the topics that He includes should be an important element in all of our times of prayer.

Other Instructions about Prayer

Although the Model Prayer is a significant example of acceptable prayer, Jesus taught about and modeled prayer in almost everything that He did or said. He walked with the Father; He depended on the Father. He listened to the Father, and taught about Him. His life revolved around loving and doing the will of His Father. This is the most important lesson that we can learn: our focus, too, should be on our relationship with the Father, with the Son, and with the Holy Spirit. Prayer is a matter of with Whom we are walking and talking...not just what we are saying or hearing.

Jesus taught much on prayer in order that we, too, would know what it involves. Some of the things that He taught are seen in the verses that I have selected for us to study. These are not all there are, of course, but they are good examples, as we try to learn how to pray more effectively.

1. Jesus taught that we should always pray and never give up, that we should ask and keep on asking, seek and keep on seeking, and knock and keep on knocking. (Lk. 18:1; Mt. 7:7, Amp.N.T.) *Persistent* and *consistent* are two good words to keep in mind as we pray. We are not persistent because we want to talk God into answering us. We are fighting against principalities and powers that are trying to keep the will of God from being done in our lives, and in the lives of others. Consistent...never giving up...is important, since God is depending on us to be channels of blessings in our world. Spiritual warfare is great; it takes time for us to win spiritual battles. And it takes time for us to understand and to submit to the will of God.

2. *Having faith in the truth of God is necessary for our prayers to be answered.* "*If you believe, you will receive whatever you ask for in prayer.*" (Mt 21:22) Does this mean that if I truly believe that God is going to give me a gold Cadillac, then He is obligated to do so? Most of us know that this perspective is not true. But sometimes when we pray for someone's healing, we tend to think that if we believe God is going to heal the person, then He is obligated to do so...because we are 'claiming the promise' that is given in this verse. The key to understanding this promise is the word 'believe.' Merriam-Webster dictionary defines the word this way: "to consider to be true or honest."[6] *The key for prayer to work is believing what God says that we should believe.* If He tells us that He will heal someone who is ill, then we can believe that, and ask for it to happen. It is like a father who tells his son that he will be home at 5:00 p.m., and will give him the keys to the family car that he can take to his school football game. Because the son believes what the father told him, at 5:00 p.m., he is at the door when his dad arrives home. He meets him and 'asks him for the keys.' He believed what the father said, but if he did not ask his father for the keys, and accept them from him, he would not be able to drive the car! We believe...we ask...God answers... we receive.

    If the son had decided to also ask for $100 to take with him to the game, believing that his father would give it to

---

[6] <u>Merriam-Webster Dictionary</u>, merriam-webster.com

him, he may have been disappointed! He believed it, but his dad had not promised it. The father thought it best not to grant the son's request for the money, no matter how much he wanted the money.

It is important that we understand what the Lord actually says to us...before we try to use this verse when we want God to do something!

3. In the Model Prayer, Jesus taught about temptation and the devil, but He also mentioned the necessity of praying as an important way to keep us from falling into temptation. We must remember that the 'flesh is weak.' Although we might prefer to blame Satan every time we sin, we are quite capable of constructing ideas on how to sin, without his help! Our flesh, our old nature, is naturally predisposed to sinning; in other words, it is our natural, default position. It is natural for us to want to 'be god.' We want to be in control of our lives, our circumstances, and our future. We usually don't realize just how weak and vulnerable we are, inclined by nature to turn our backs on God. Many times, we don't see this human weakness and vulnerability until we fall into temptation and sin. "Pray that you will not fall into temptation," Jesus instructed. (Lk. 22:40). But we often fail to do this, much to our detriment.

4. Jesus also told His disciples that they must pray for their enemies, for those who persecuted them. (Mt. 5:44) Why would He tell them to do such a hard thing? Doesn't He realize how hard it is for us to even like some people, much less those who actually do us harm? We don't have to wonder why...He told us why in the verses that follow these words of instruction: (a) That is what children of the King do;

(b) God blesses the unrighteous and the righteous with rain and sunshine. We need to bless the unrighteous by praying for them; (c) Christians should be behaving at least as well as pagans do; (d) Our goal is to be as perfect as God is. Why should we pray for our enemies? Jesus told us to do so!

5. Another word of instruction that Jesus taught is found in Mk. 11:24. "Whatever you ask for in prayer, believe that you have received it, and it will be yours." Good. I can now ask for that Cadillac!

What is Jesus teaching here? It sounds as if I can decide on what I want, and if I truly believe that I have gotten it already, then it is mine. Note the part of the verse that says, 'you *have received* it,' because this phrase is the key to understanding what Jesus is teaching here about prayer.

Let's look at something Jesus said that is recorded in John 14:27. "Peace I leave with you; my peace *I give you*." We *'have received'* peace. When we 'believe' that Jesus has already left His peace here for us, because He said that He did, then we can ask for it… and receive it, through prayer.

Suppose you are a teenager, and your mother texted you that she went shopping during the day while you were in school. She told you that she bought a pair of shoes that you had been wanting. When you arrive home from school, because you believed what your mother told you, you go to her and ask her to give you what you believe is yours… the new shoes. You ask, because she told you that she bought them…and you believed her. But, you still had to choose whether or not to accept what was promised to you.

Jesus told us to search the Bible to see what is written there…what He has already given to us. When we 'believe,' we can then go to Him in prayer to receive it! I wonder how many 'spiritual shoes' are left unclaimed!

What Did Jesus Pray?

Jesus modeled prayer; we have looked at some examples of that. He taught us to pray; we have seen some of those instructions. But what did Jesus actually SAY when He talked with His Father? Jesus' prayers to the Father are interesting and informative. There is so much to learn from a study of exactly what He voiced in prayer.

1. *"I praise you, Father, Lord of heaven and earth, because You have hidden these things from the wise and learned, and revealed them to little children. Yes, Father, for this was your good pleasure."* (Mt. 11:25-26). Here are a few things that I think we can learn from this spoken prayer by Jesus:

    a. He knows the importance of praising His Father. So should we.

    b. He addressed God as His Father. This showed intimacy. And yet, He said that God is 'Lord of heaven and earth.' We need to have a balance in our prayers, as well as in our theology. God is indeed our Father, but He is also the Lord of heaven and earth.

    c. Depending on man's wisdom and knowledge can actually keep us from hearing the truths that God wants to impart. It is so important to be trusting and teachable, humble and open like little children are.

2. *"Father, I thank you that you have heard me. I knew that you always hear me, but I said this for the benefit of the*

people standing here, that they may believe that you sent me." (John 11:41-42) Jesus is praying at the tomb of Lazarus. What can we learn from this prayer?

    a. We need to always thank God for hearing our prayers, and at times to address Him as 'Father'.

    b. Sometimes the prayer that we pray in the presence of others is for their benefit. They can be influenced to believe, when they hear belief in God uttered by us in prayer.

    c. Prayer can and does empower us to do mighty things for God.

3. *"Father, glorify your name."* (John 12:28) What a wonderful prayer that should be included in every prayer we pray to God. Jesus is obviously demonstrating here the same advice He gave to His disciples in the Model Prayer: *"Hallowed be your name."* We can never go wrong in offering this kind of prayer!

4. *"My Father, if it is possible, may this cup pass from me. Yet not as I will, but as you will."* (Mt. 26:38) We find additional instructions about prayer in this passage. Jesus is in the Garden of Gethsemane. His disciples are asleep, instead of watching and praying, as Jesus had instructed them to do. I think that there are a few important lessons to learn from this prayer by Jesus, the one that He voiced during one of the most difficult times of His earthly life.

    a. We see again His intimacy with God. He addressed Him once again as 'Father.' This is a Son who is asking for help from His Father. We need to have that same attitude when we talk with God. This is our Father with Whom we are talking. He is the One who knows us, and loves us, and He always wants the best for us. We are not addressing a king who does not know us, and who is so busy running the universe that He does not have time to deal with us.

b. Jesus is specific, but humble, about His request. He is not demanding His own way. He is sharing the painful situation with His Father, to ask if there is some way that He can be spared the anguish of what He knows He will soon face. We, too, need to approach God in humility with our requests. We must be specific about what we want Him to do, or to keep us from having to face. It is not acceptable to bargain with God, or to demand our own way.

c. Jesus submitted His will to the will of the Father. He trusted that the Father knew what was best, what was possible, what was permissible. Although Jesus struggled three times in his prayers to God, He always ended them with a submission to the will and wisdom of God. This, too, must be the way that we pray. We can acknowledge our pain, and our preferences for what we want to happen. But we must always trust that the Father's way is best. We must submit our will to His will.

5. Jesus prayed three prayers while hanging on the cross: *(1) "Father, forgive them; for they do not know what they are doing."* (Lk. 23:34); (2) *"My God, my God, why have you forsaken me?"* (Mt. 27:46); (3) *"Father, into your hands I commit my spirit."* (Lk. 23:46) What can we learn from these prayers that can help us in our own prayers?

a. It is important that we ask the Father to forgive those who have done evil against us. Stephen was able to do this as he was being stoned to death. (Acts 7:60) You may wonder how Stephen was able to do this. The Bible provides the answer: he was a man *'full of faith and of the Holy Spirit.'* (Acts 6:5) *'He was full of God's grace and power, and did great wonders among the people.'* (Acts 6:8) There is the answer. He couldn't pray such a prayer for his enemies in his own strength; neither can we. But when we are full of faith and the Holy Spirit, we will have the strength to obey God, and to even pray for those who harm us.

b. It is OK to cry out to God in prayer when we feel isolated and abandoned by Him. But those times of desperation do not last, if we allow the Lord to help us. Jesus cried out. But God strengthened Him and restored His trust. He will do the same for us.

c. Placing our lives and our concerns into the Father's hands should be an integral part of our prayers. He is the only one who can do anything about them, and He always does what is best. He is trustworthy. He is our loving Father.

The longest recorded prayer of Jesus is found in the gospel of John, Chapter 17. He is interceding for His disciples and for us. Let's look at some of the things that He prayed about to His Father, and consider what we can learn that will help us in our own prayer life.

Jesus Prays for His Disciples and for Us: John 17

It is always comforting to me to know when people are praying for me. If they tell me what they are praying, or pray with me, or send me a copy of their prayers, it is even more of a blessing. John 17 is such a wonderful glimpse into the prayer life of Jesus. It brings encouragement to us to read it, not only to learn what He prayed for His disciples (who were with Him at that time), but it is also wonderful to know that He also included us! *"My prayer is not for them alone. I pray also for those who will believe in me through their message, that all of them may be one, Father, just as you are in me and I am in you."* (John 17:30-31) We see what He prayed for them then, and we realize that He is still praying these things for us! This study can also help us to be wiser in our own prayers.

Some of the requests that Jesus made to His Father are as follows:

Vs 11, 15: For protection from the evil one.

Vs 17: Sanctification by the truth (to be set apart and made holy by truth)

Vs 18: To send them out into the world

Vs 21-23: To be brought to complete unity that the world may know and recognize God.

Vs 26: That the love that God has for Jesus may be in us, and that Jesus will be in us.

There are only a handful of prayers by Jesus that are recorded in the Bible. This one in John 17 is the longest. Obviously, what He prayed should be the type of requests we make when we talk with the Father. One of the most important ones that I noticed is the **request for protection** from Satan. I think that we often fail to pray such a request for ourselves and for others. Most of the time, we would rather not think about our enemy, and about the fact that he desires to harm us. He hates God, and therefore, we are also on his 'hate-list.' What better way to hurt God than to hurt us? He does not want us to have communication and fellowship with God, nor does he want us to be successful in spreading the good news about salvation. We are engaged in spiritual warfare, and probably are not winning as many battles as we could, and should.

Another thing we read about in John 17 is that Jesus prayed for us to **be sanctified,** to be made holy. I don't think that we pray this request very often, either. We need to pray for God's Spirit to continue to work with us, convincing us of the need to walk with the Lord in holiness of life, thought, and speech, every day! As we become convinced, we should ask Him to transform us and other believers into the very image of our holy Lord Himself. One of the ways that Satan disrupts our fellowship with God is by leading us into sin and disobedience, creating a blockage between us and our Holy Lord. We need to realize that it is a spiritual blessing to be convicted of sin by the Spirit. We should pray that He convict us whenever we, and those for whom we pray, step out of the will and fellowship of God. And we need His help to take the necessary steps to become reconciled with God once again.

Another theme that surfaces in Jesus' prayer, recorded in John 17, is His request **that there be unity among believers**. We seem to be ignorant regarding the importance of unity. One of the main results of such unity is the positive message that it sends to the lost world. Jesus reminds us that unity is so unusual, when people see it, it will cause them to look at why it is happening. When we love one another, it gets people's attention...in a positive way. When we fuss and argue, it distracts others from our main message to the world. It gets their attention when we fuss. But it leads them away from God, instead of to Him. Do we pray enough for unity in our churches? Are we praying for unity in families, offices, and in our world?

Another important topic that Jesus mentioned in His prayer was that **believers be sent out into the world.** Unbelievers need to hear about the good news, in order for them to have fellowship with the One who loved them enough to die for their sins. Jesus also told His disciples to plead to the Lord of the harvest to send out laborers into the harvest. I wonder how differently our world would be if we were faithful to pray that prayer?

Some Lessons from Jesus' Prayers

A close study of Jesus' prayer life soon reveals some important truths that we should learn and practice, as we try to grow in our relationship with God through prayer.

1. **Prayer is absolutely necessary**. If the Son of God felt the need, and had the desire to commune with His Father, why do we think that we can get along without it?

2. **We can pray in public and 'on the run,' but it is also important for us to have times when we are alone with God**. These times of drawing aside to spend time with the Lord should be often. They are especially needed when we are seeking direction, or comfort, or strength.

3. **Prayer can sometimes be hard work**. Satan is at work, the flesh (old nature) pulls us down and away from God, and the world is both distracting and demanding. If we are convinced of the importance of prayer and communing with our Lord, then we will make any sacrifice necessary to be successful at it. Our main difficulty may be the reality that we aren't really convinced of the urgency of prayer!

4. **We need to pray specifically and with purpose**. Our prayers should never be done out of habit, with no 'heart' involvement. Using a list can be helpful for intercession, but it should never limit our prayers. And it should not be used if it, in any way, distracts us from the sheer joy of communing with the One who loves us. You would not be happy if a loved-one only wanted to be around you when they wanted you to do things that they had written on a list!

I have even seen this principle played out between my dogs and me. Of course, I am happy to respond when they come to me, asking for their supper. I comply, even when it is not convenient for me, because I love them, and they need me. But it is so much more joyful when they come to me, and just want to be with me! We can learn from them, to be sure.[7]

5. **We must believe that prayer works, and is worth taking the time to do.** Of course, it is wonderful when we see the results of our prayers, or when someone tells us that they could feel our prayers. But we need to be convinced that something actually happens each time we go to the throne of grace, even when we are not aware of it. I plant little seeds each spring. I don't get discouraged when I don't see the results of my efforts during the first few weeks after the planting. But I know that something is happening, even when I cannot see it. I have learned that the Lord often lets us see or hear how our prayers are working…just frequently enough to encourage us, but not so often for us to become proud!

6. **Prayer is necessary to keep us in God's will.** We stray. We have our own preferences. Staying in tune with God daily, through prayer and worship, goes a long way to help us know and to do His will each day. We can voice our 'preferences' to God, our concerns about what we might have to face, etc. But there must always be the attitude of 'not my will, but His will be done' if we want to remain safely in His will. It is the only sure way to complete His purpose for us.

Prayer always strengthens us and those for whom we pray. The source of spiritual power is prayer. Why do we

---

[7] For more lessons on what you can learn from your pets, purchase a copy of Furry Philosophy: What We Learned from our Four-Legged Friends, Cullinan and Sears, amazon.com or lamplighters-ministries.org.

choose to remain so weak? When we listen to God in prayer, we will gain strength, as well as obtain wisdom and direction. Why do we choose to remain confused or weak? Once we make a commitment to pray, we should do everything in our power to learn how to do it correctly. We must study what the Bible teaches, read books that others have written, and talk with other believers, all of which can be helpful. But the best thing we can do is to actually pray…to spend time talking, listening, and loving on our precious Lord.

Who Else in the Bible Gave Helpful Advice on Prayer?

Paul definitely was a man of prayer. His letters are filled with helpful advice, and in those same letters are examples of prayers that he prayed for the churches and individuals to whom he was writing. What are some things that we can learn from a study of Paul's prayer life?

1. We are to be unceasing and persistent in prayer, and to give thanks in all circumstances. We are not told to be thankful FOR all things…but to be thankful that God is in the midst of all things with us. (I Thess. 5:16-18) These things are actually the will of God for us, Paul writes.

You may wonder how you can 'pray without ceasing.' Obviously, we cannot be talking, or even focusing on God, every waking moment. We have other things that demand our attention and time. Another example from my dogs might help us understand what Paul is getting at in these verses. My pups love to be where I am. They sleep a lot, probably because I sit a lot! But, whenever I move, they move. If I try to slip out of the room, even when I think that they are asleep, I find them right behind me…even following me into the bathroom! They seem to be 'tuned in to me', no matter what I am doing. They may open one eyelid to see what I am up to, but they know if I leave or stay in the room where they are. That 'watchful attitude' should be our mind-set. We should be so aware of God's presence, that when He moves, we move. When He speaks, we hear. When we need Him or want to share something with Him, it is no big deal. We are aware that He is right there with us.

2. Paul reminds us that we are told not to be anxious about anything, but to pray about everything. We are instructed to offer our various prayers and petitions to God, but to be sure that they are all wrapped up in prayers of thanksgiving. The result will be peace that passes all understanding, peace which will guard our hearts and minds. (Phil. 4:4-9)

Let's think for a few moments about what that looks like. We can ask God to show us the decision we should make in a certain situation we are facing. We offer the petition, and then we wrap it up in thanksgiving:

> **The petition**: *Lord, I have this decision that must be made by the end of the week, and I don't know the wisest thing to do. I am confused and need to hear from You. My two choices are: (mention them). Please speak to my heart and guide my thoughts.*
>
> **Thanksgiving**: *Thank You, Lord, because I know that You are going to let me know which decision is the wisest one. I praise You for the guidance You will give to me. I will listen and think and wait for your peace to assure me that*

I am doing the right thing. Thank you, Lord, because I can count on You again.

3. We must ask the Spirit to help us pray, and then allow Him to pray for us and through us. (Rom. 8:26-27) Most of us realize that we need help praying. We don't know what to say or how to offer our prayers as we should. And probably most of all, we really don't take the time to do it! Thankfully, God was gracious enough to give to us the Holy Spirit to live inside of us. We need inside help, not just outside suggestions! So, we can ask the Spirit to help us to pray, to remind us to pray, to pray for us, and to pray through us. This is something that we absolutely must keep in mind if we want to make progress in our desire to be people who pray effectively.

4. We are to pray all kinds of prayers and requests. (Phil. 4:4) We must work to keep our prayer lives balanced, being sure to include all types of prayer...and being certain to listen to God, of course. If we simply confess, but don't claim God's promises, we lose out on joy. If we petition while neglecting praise and thanksgiving, we can become selfish. If we only intercede, but don't spend time communing with God, we miss out on personal peace which His presence provides.

5. We must be alert against Satan's tricks and attacks, and to keep on praying for all the saints everywhere. (Eph. 6:18). We need to 'watch each other's backs.' Satan is on the move. He wants to hurt believers, to rob them of joy and purpose. He wants to keep us distracted, so that we fail to share God's word with others. He wants to keep us fighting with each other, to keep us from having time or energy to fight him. He wants to lead us into sin in order to ruin our witness. He wants to split churches, so he can laugh in God's face. We must pray. We must fight. We must wear the armor of God.

It is the Spirit's power within us that brings forth more blessings than we can ever imagine! How is that done? Through prayer…all of it… every day…in every situation.

When will we do what is clearly taught in the Bible concerning prayer? Why do we continue to rob ourselves of the blessings that God has provided for us?

What James Taught About Prayer

The Apostle James also reminds us of the power available to us through prayer. Chapter 5 of his letter gives us valuable insight into how much he believed in the power of prayer. He said to 'pray when in trouble'; to 'praise when happy'; 'to pray when there is sickness'; 'to confess our sins'. He also said that we have the same power available to us that Elijah did when he prayed about the weather. He reminds us that there is great power available in prayer when a person is 'righteous': right with God and with others. Do we believe what James wrote? Do we realize the potential power of prayer that we are failing to utilize? The question that rings in my mind at this point of our discussion is the same one that Jesus asked: "Why do you call me Lord, Lord, and do not do what I say?" (Luke 6:46) Although the context of this comment by Jesus is not dealing with the topic of prayer, it certainly fits. He could have phrased the question like this: "Why do you call me Lord, Lord, and fail to spend time with me in prayer?" I wonder how you would answer Jesus. We know that we should pray more. Why don't we?

Is There Really Power in Prayer?

If we were given a survey about our opinion about prayer, and on it was a question asking if we thought that there is great power in prayer, I believe that most of us would answer 'Yes.' There may be a few skeptics out there, but I believe that most Christians believe that prayer is powerful. The problem arises, however, when we consider whether or not we have ever been the person who prayed, and powerful results occurred. We may have felt the prayers of others, but do we feel that WE are ever the reason for these 'power-felt' comments? Let's take a few moments to look at what the Bible teaches about *power in prayer*, and then consider how we can experience more powerful praying.

James tells us in Chapter 5, verse 16 (Amp. N.T.) that *"The earnest, heartfelt, continued prayer of a righteous man makes tremendous power available, dynamic in its working."* Tremendous power. Dynamic in its working. James believed in the power of prayer. He had obviously seen powerful praying, when he observed Jesus pray. And he was in the upper room, where those assembled 'devoted themselves steadfastly to prayer.' (Acts 1:14) The power of the Holy Spirit came at Pentecost, probably at least in part because of their prayers. He witnessed the power of the resurrection of Jesus, being one of the people to whom Jesus appeared. (I Cor.15:7). He heard and believed Paul's report of how the Spirit had also fallen on the Gentiles, and he responded favorably. He obviously was not surprised when he saw the power of prayer, and the dynamic presence of God's Spirit.

Note some of the other evidence in his letter that indicates his belief in the power of prayer. In chapter 1, for instance, he wrote: *"If any of you lacks wisdom, he should ask God, who gives generously to all without finding fault, and it will be given to him."* (Vs. 5) Other evidence of James' appreciation of prayer, in its various forms, is seen in the following verses:

"With the tongue, we praise our Lord..." (3:9)

"You do not have, because you do not ask God." (4:3)

"Come near to God, and He will come near to you." (4:8)

"Humble yourselves before the Lord, and he will lift you up." (4:10)

"The cries of the harvesters have reached the ears of the Lord Almighty." (5:4)

What are some other verses in the Bible that emphasize the power of prayer? Consider the following:

"After they prayed, the place where they were meeting was shaken. And they were all filled with the Holy Spirit and spoke the word of God boldly." (Acts 4:31)

"I prayed for this child, and the Lord has granted me what I asked of Him." (I Sam. 1:27)

"From inside the fish, Jonah prayed." (Jonah 2:1)

"So we fasted and petitioned our God about this, and he answered our prayer." (Ezra 8:23)

"The Lord accepts my prayer." (Ps. 6:9)

"The eyes of the Lord are on the righteous and his ears are attentive to their prayer." (I Peter 3:12)

Evidence of the Spirit's Power Because of the Prayers of the Early Church:

1. Acts 2:4   All were diffused, throughout their souls, with the Spirit. All manifested God in some way beyond their own ability. Others were astonished and bewildered and amazed. They told of the mighty works of God.

2. Acts 2:13   Their behavior made some laugh, make a joke, and try to explain away what they saw.

3. Acts 2: 14   They had to explain to others what was going on.

4. Acts 2:18   Gender barriers were erased. Men and women were prophesying events pertaining to God's kingdom.

5. Acts 2:37, 41   Conviction and conversion of those who observed their worship. People came to see for themselves what was going on.

6. Acts 2:42   Bible study…preaching, as well as a sense of loyalty and fellowship; and prayer were the main focus.

7. Acts 2:43   Awe and miraculous answers to prayer happened.

8. Acts 2:45   Unity.

9. Acts 2:46   Fellowship outside the walls of the church.

10. Acts 2:47   Great joy.

11. Acts 2:48   Much praise of God.

12. Acts 2:49   People being saved on a daily basis.

Most Christians, who are walking with the Lord, and are praying on a regular basis, don't have to be convinced that prayer makes a difference. Because the Spirit lives within us, there is tremendous power available as He prays for and through us. Our responsibility is to be available to Him, and to keep ourselves cleansed. It is urgent that we remember that "The power is in the ONE who hears, not in the one who prays it; therefore, prayers are powerful." [8]

---

[8] Max Lucado, source unknown.

Key 5:

Understand the Role of the Holy Spirit

Have you ever wondered why the Holy Spirit was sent to us? What did Jesus say were the reasons that the Spirit was sent to earth to inhabit believers? And what is His role, if any, in helping us to pray effectively? One of the major reasons our prayers are not as effective as they should be, is probably our misunderstanding of the role of the Holy Spirit in prayer.

What Jesus Said About the Holy Spirit

Can you imagine how you would feel if you were to look outside on the morning of your birthday to discover a huge present in your driveway? It is a brand new, very expensive, sports car sitting there, with a huge red ribbon on it. And when you walk outside for a closer view, you find a large birthday card, with your name on it, attached to the windshield of the car. You open the card to discover that the car is your present from someone you know, who can afford to give it to you. What would your reaction be? You may wonder why the person decided to give the car to you. You may even wonder if it is all a joke, that it is not really a present for you, after all. Or you may be skeptical about whether the person expects something in return, or that you will be required to pay them back for the gift.

After you do get all of your questions and doubts answered, you discover that indeed the present is yours to keep, with no strings attached. What would your reaction likely be? Ecstatic, overwhelming joy... most likely. And you would certainly enjoy your gift, and would let others know about your good fortune.

It is really important that we learn how to recognize the wonderful gifts that God Himself has given to us, and to react in ecstatic, overwhelming joy when we realize just what these gifts are. He has given many good gifts to us, but one of them is especially, according to Jesus; the precious gift of His Spirit. Have you ever wondered why we were given this wonderful gift? Why do we need Him? Does the Bible give us any answers about why we were presented with such a glorious gift? Thankfully, Jesus told us the reasons for such a gift. We learn about it in the Scripture, God's Word to us.

Jesus told His disciples that He was going away. But He said that He would send 'Another...to be with them forever.' This gift would be 'Another... just like Himself.' His disciples needed Jesus' presence and power; and so do we. And there are many reasons why we need the Spirit. Jesus told us some of these reasons:

1. *He will counsel you and guide you into all truth.* (John 14:16)

Life is confusing, filled with decisions to make, and problems to overcome. Even the Bible is sometimes difficult to understand. Google has changed the world for many of us, putting bookstores out of business, making encyclopedias and libraries less enticing, and even eliminating the need for huge phone directories. The world of information has invaded our lives. Phones and iPads and iWatches connect us to information that was never quite as accessible as it is now. Single-purpose cameras have been replaced, for the most part. And there are people who do not even remember that we used to have to take a roll of film to the store to have it developed. Even with all of this readily available information, we are still confused about so many things. The Holy Spirit is vital to the Christian. Our lives depend on His guidance.

2. *He will teach you and remind you of everything I have said to you.* (John 14:26)

When I was a professor, I became aware of just how many students needed tutors to help them pass their classes. Personal explanation and review of the subject matter was what they needed to be equipped to succeed. The Holy Spirit is the Christian's tutor. He teaches each of us what we need to know, and He does it in such a way that it helps us, no matter where we are in our walk as a Christian. He does not attempt to teach us calculus, when we are working on our multiplication tables! He knows our capabilities and our personalities. And, if we have trouble remembering what we have already studied, He will run that lesson by us again! I like the fact that He 'reminds us of what Jesus said to us.'

Don't forget to thank the Lord for your personal tutor, and to listen carefully to what He is attempting to teach you.

3. *He will testify about me.* (John 15:26)

One thing I have noticed, since joining the Facebook community, is how easy it is to discover what someone's passions are. In other words, if a person is a Carolina Panthers or Clemson fan, you can expect to see their 'postings' contain a great deal of information about their favorite team. And you will notice pictures taken at a game, and t-shirts with their favorite team name on them. If they are fishermen or beach-goers, that is what their Facebook posts will discuss. And you will also see pictures of pets and grandchildren, posted by those whose happiness is found in these relationships.

If the Holy Spirit had a Facebook account, I wonder who would be in His posts. You can guess the answer from the above Scripture. The Spirit's pictures and conversation would be centered on Jesus. He absolutely loves to elevate Jesus, to talk about Him, and to teach about Him, in order to draw people to Him. I think it would be wise for us to learn how to do the same things! If you want more of the Holy Spirit's presence in your life or church, spend time elevating and praising Jesus, and watch what happens!

4. *He will convict the world of guilt in regard to sin and righteousness and judgment.* (John 16:8)

Before we approach the throne of grace in prayer, we should always ask the Holy Spirit to search our hearts, and to convict us of anything that might hinder our prayers. When we pray, we are walking into the presence of a Holy God. We must not try to do so until we are cleansed of our sins. Since we are masters of self-deception, always thinking about how well we are doing in our relationship with God, it is always best to ask the Spirit to show us what we cannot see in our own lives. It is not fun to be convicted of failing to live up to the Lord's standards, but it is necessary. We will not confess what we do not see! We should thank the Spirit for His role in showing us these problem areas.

5. *He will speak only what He hears, and he will tell you what is to come.* (John 16:13)

When I was teaching at Gardner-Webb University, I taught at class about religious cults and the occult. One of the optional assignments I gave to the students was a choice to visit a fortune teller. I was careful to guide the students about whom to select, since I was aware of a demonic presence among some practitioners. It seems to be so enticing for some people to seek out information about the future from those who claim to have that ability. I also took the students to bookstores, and asked them to peruse the section on the occult. It was shocking what they discovered...a large number of albums whose covers contained images of demons, devils, and even Satan!

Among cultic trends today is a widespread desire to know what is going to happen in the future. According to a 2016 survey about paranormal beliefs conducted by Chapman University, "14.1% of those surveyed believe astrologers, fortune tellers and psychics can foresee the future."[9]

Most of the time, it is best not to know what the future holds for us. But there are times when we DO need to have some information about the future. It is at those times that the Spirit will let us know "what is to come." It may simply be an impression that something in the future will be favorable. At other times, He can give us a glimpse, a vision if you

---

[9] https://www.mic.com/articles/161389/here-s-why-people-keep-going-to-psychics-and-fortunetellers

please, of how something is going to turn out for us. When we need to know something, even if it involves peeking through the curtain between the present and the future, we can be assured that the Holy Spirit will do that for the child of God who is walking with the Lord.

6. *He will bring glory to me by taking what is mine and making it known to you.* (John 16:14)

One day recently, I was cleaning out closets. I found some letters that I didn't even know I had. My mother had kept several letters that my father had written to her over 60 years ago! Many of them were written even before I was born. It was intriguing to read them, and at times to feel as though I was overhearing him speak those words to my mother. I learned facts about both of them that I did not know before I read the letters. Not only did I learn some interesting tidbits of information, I was able to get a glimpse into their hearts. Words of love and endearment were shared between them, as well as painful emotions they shared about issues that were challenging them.

One of the wonderful things that the Spirit does for us is to interpret the Lord's love-letters to us. He lets us know what Jesus said, and how He lived. But the Spirit also reveals the heart of Jesus to us... how He felt then, and how He feels now... about us. He lets us know when we hurt Jesus, and He delivers personal messages that Jesus has for us. Often, when we pray to the Lord, it is the Spirit who gives us the answers for which we seek.

Notice the first part of the verse in this section: "He will bring glory to me." To bring glory means two things: (1) to honor, and (2) to reveal the essence of. The Spirit will always lift up and honor Jesus, and He will reveal to us the beauty of the Savior. How does He do that? Jesus said that one of the ways that the Spirit will do that is by "taking what is mine and making it known to you." The Holy Spirit is the One who will let us know just how wonderful Jesus really is! And when we get a glimpse of Jesus, how can we NOT want to spend time in prayer... loving and being loved by Him!

The Spirit and our Prayers

The following information about the Holy Spirit is important to us as we try to learn how to pray more effectively.

1. He will teach us what the will of God is for us, what we should pray for, and how to do so.

One of the main ways that He will do this is when we read and study God's Word. I have also learned from my own times of prayer and worship, that if an impression from Him enters my mind, it often helps me with questions I may have. And, sometimes, a person will come to my mind, or I may remember something that I forgot to do. More than likely, you have had this happen to you. And often accompanying the thought is a prompting to pray, or to do something...like calling the person. These 'sudden and sometimes unexpected' thoughts may be God's Spirit prompting us to meet a need in someone's life. We should do our best to be sensitive and responsive to these impressions. And, even if they originate from our own minds, it never hurts to pray for or to call someone!

2. He will remind us of what Jesus taught about prayer, and will help us pray effectively.

One of the greatest blessings I experience is having Bible verses flood into my mind. Just this morning, as I was journaling a passage in Isaiah, the Spirit brought to my mind several other related passages on the topic which I was studying. He seems to reach into the concordance of my mind, calling verses to my attention! Because He usually does not give me the location of the verses, I just laugh and look them up in a Bible concordance.

It is especially a blessing when the Spirit brings a Bible verse or promise to my mind when I am struggling with something in prayer.

3. He will help us keep Jesus as the focus of all of our prayers, helping us to remember to keep the praise of Jesus at the center of all of our prayers.

One of the reasons I love to begin my day with music and worship (even before I pray or study the Bible), is because music helps me to focus on Jesus. I am careful to select songs that are about Him, and which express my love to Him. I try to do this before I select other songs to play. Praising Him releases the Spirit's power to me... and through me as I pray for others.

4. He will faithfully convict us of our own sin and disobedience, because of how sin blocks the effectiveness of our prayers.

Most of us don't want to feel God's conviction; it is too painful. As we grow in our relationship with the Lord, however, we will become more thankful for the faithfulness of the Spirit to reveal our sin. My pups don't like to be told that they have to 'go into the sink' for a bath or a footwashing, before they can have full fellowship with me and my beige carpet! But, when they are clean, they seem to forget the short time they were alienated from me.

Once we experience the joy of full fellowship with the Lord, and have seen the power of the Spirit in answering our prayers, we will be less likely to shrink back from the Spirit's conviction. Instead, we will willingly ask Him to turn the search light upon us, to help us see where we need to ask for cleansing.

Last week, we had an unusual experience with the pups. It is something I had never experienced in all of my many years of owning pups. They were SKUNKED! Early one morning, they barked for me to let them outside. They have free-run of the portion of the yard that is fenced in for them. But a skunk had gotten into the yard, and the pups went running after it. Even though I hollered for them to stop, they were determined to chase it. You can probably guess what happened next. The skunk turned around and sprayed them! Needless to say, they did NOT have full fellowship with me and my beige carpet, until some serious washing took place! Even a week later, they and the house still reeked of a slight smell of skunk-perfume! Hopefully, none of us will ever get into so much sin that there is a lingering 'smell' that offends God, us and others!

5. He will help us glorify Jesus in our prayers and with our lives, and will constantly remind us just how wonderful the Savior is.

I learned many years ago just how much the Spirit loves to elevate Jesus. It will help us tremendously if we remember that fact. It is easy for us to get caught up in our own problems and prayers for ourselves and others, and fail to think about or to thank Jesus for who He is to us. It is so important for us to remember the role that the Spirit plays in our prayers. We need to always ask for His power and direction, His conviction, teaching and guidance...as we pray, and as we read the Bible.

How Does Prayer Work When the Spirit is in Control?

I am suspicious (although I have never really asked people, or taken an opinion poll) that most of us don't think much about the role of the Spirit in making our prayer lives more effective. Many people are probably like I was as a new Christian: trying to think of the right way to SAY something in the form of a prayer that will be acceptable to God. And, of course, we want our prayer to make sense to those who might hear us praying. But what we SAY is not really that important. We may do our most effective praying when we don't actually say anything! How is that true? Basically, the role of the Spirit in prayer is to pray FOR us and THROUGH us.

> *In the same way, the Spirit helps us in our weakness. We do not know what we ought to pray for, but the Spirit himself intercedes for us with groans that words cannot express. And he who searches our hearts knows the mind of the Spirit, because the Spirit intercedes for the saints in accordance with God's will.* (Rom. 8:26)

The Spirit knows what to pray for; we do not always have to know. He always prays according to God's will, so

His prayers are always answered. We should ask Him to pray for us, and to pray through us. I find that it is easier for me to allow Him to do the praying through me, if I do two things: (1) Play music that helps me worship, and (2) visualize the person for whom I am praying. In my mind, I either hold them up to God to bless, or I visualize my holding a tube or pipe that is pointed to heaven and is extended to the person for whom I am praying. I say nothing. I just silently pray that He flow through me to provide the person with what they need. And if I am praying for myself, I just 'connect to God' and ask that He do in me and for me what I need. At times, I ask Him to bring people to my mind, so that I can 'send them a little prayer-juice' (as I like to express the concept to my friends). It really does help to intercede or petition in this way. It seems to give the Spirit room to pray the prayers or send the power in ways that are according to God's will. Sometimes, I visualize myself standing before the glory of heaven, much like one would stand out in the sunshine. I look to heaven, and allow the 'sunshine of His glory' to flow down upon me, or upon the person for whom I am praying. An important thing to remember, however, for when you use either of these approaches: The Spirit needs cleansed vessels through whom to work.

    I think back to the time when I wanted to use weed killer on my yard. I purchased a tank sprayer in order to be able to mix up concentrated weed killer to use. After I mixed the water and concentrate, I repeatedly pumped the handle on the tank, in order for the pressure to build up. I pointed the hose toward the weeds, and pulled the trigger. Nothing happened. I tried to pump more pressure, but it was at capacity. The problem? The tip of the hose was clogged with dirt. When I discovered the problem and cleaned the nozzle, out came a strong flow of the mixed water and chemical.

Such it is with the flow of the Holy Spirit in prayer. If my life is clogged with unconfessed sin of any kind, no matter how small, the power is hindered and the flow is blocked. Repentance and confession will clear away the hindrances, allowing the Spirit to accomplish God's will through me when I pray.

The Spirit plays a key role in our lives. He is the one who convicted us that we needed Jesus, and He drew us to the Savior. He is the one who 'birthed us' into the family of God, when we trusted Christ to be our Savior and Lord. He is the one who indwells us, who has gifted us for service, and who fills us with the fruit of the Spirit. He counsels us, teaches us, uses us, and prays for and through us. It would do us well to study more about Him, in order to be as effective as possible as prayer warriors in the family of God.

What Did Paul Say About the Holy Spirit and Prayer?

Paul was obviously a person of prayer, a child of God from whom we can learn a great deal about the Spirit's role in prayer. Paul spent many days in jail or prison, arrested because of his faithfulness to preach the good news about Jesus. Because many of his letters were penned while he was in jail, he often used 'soldier' analogies to get across spiritual truths. One important passage about the Spirit and prayer is found in Ephesians 6. He is writing from a prison cell in Rome. He knows by personal experience just how fierce the warfare is between the forces of evil and the forces of good. He understood the powers of darkness, as well as the potential power available for doing good. He knew how important prayer is, and he wrote instructions to fellow believers about how they could be better warriors on the battlefield of faith.

Paul wrote about the spiritual armor of God that Christians need, if we are to be successful against principalities and powers which seek to destroy us. He also wrote about the power necessary to wear and use the armor effectively: prayer. He also knew that the only true way to pray effectively was 'in the Spirit.' (Eph. 6:18)

One good way to understand the concept of being 'in the Spirit' is to think about riding in a car. When we are 'in' the car, wherever it goes or does not go, we go or do not go. We have some control over this, if we are the driver. But if we are not driving, we are captive to the person who is driving. Where they decide to go, we have to go, whether we like it or not. To pray 'in the Spirit' is to let Him be in control of all decisions about where and when and how we pray. We have some effect on how well that goes, of course, but we should make a commitment to 'let Him drive.' And, we need to be careful that we are not spending the entire time complaining like a back-seat driver!

Another word of instruction from Paul's writings is that our praying should be *'on all occasions,' with all kinds of prayers and requests.'* (vs. 18) This is one way in which we are a vital part of the prayer process. We need to be 'prayer-warriors,' or perhaps we could say 'prayer-passengers.' We ride along with the Spirit, and we pray how and what and when He directs. We must 'be alert,' and 'always keep praying for all the saints.' We should be alert to the Spirit for guidance, alert for Satan's attacks and tricks, and alert to the needs that fellow believers have for our prayers. We need to be 'responsible riders' in the Holy Spirit's car.

We are not to grieve the Spirit (sadden Him with our sin, disobedience, or laziness), nor are we to quench Him (snuff Him out or squelch whatever He tries to tell us, or resist how He may want to use us.) We are to be 'filled with Him,' sensitive to His promptings, and willing for Him to use us to do anything that He wants to do. And one of the main things He will do through us is to use us as channels of God's blessings to the world.

An Important Warning

We may be glad to know that Jesus gave us the Spirit, and we may be thankful for His help in our times of prayer. But one thing we often forget is our inborn tendency to run our own lives, even when it comes to spiritual matters. There is a strong independent streak in each of us. The old nature within us is determined to 'be god.' And there is no greater temptation to do this, perhaps, than in the matter of prayer. We want to be the dispenser of blessings which we choose to give. We want to make people do what we think they should do. We want to determine our own destiny, to avoid temptation and pain. We want to be well-known and well-thought of for being devout, committed, praying Christians. The problem lurking behind all of these goals, and perhaps even well-intentioned ambitions, is when we formulate our prayers as ways to control or even coerce the King of the Universe into doing what we think is best!

In one of his books, Martyn Lloyd-Jones wrote: "We must come face to face with our tendency to try to pray on our own."[10] In other words, we are usually so certain that we know what is best for us or for someone else that it is quite normal to completely ignore the Holy Spirit, and not even ask for His help and wisdom as we pray! We MUST remember to rely upon Him, or many of our prayers will simply be a waste of time. And if we grieve or quench the Spirit, while still expecting Him to have fellowship with us, we are walking in darkness. We will not sense God's presence. We will not experience answers to prayers. We will not be strengthened or empowered for service, or have strength to face our trials. We will not be able to withstand temptation or be able to stand against the onslaughts of the devil. We will not bear spiritual fruit, and our spiritual gifts will be rendered useless, or at least unproductive. We need the Spirit's presence. We need Him to guide, teach, convict and empower us. When we believe what John recorded from the lips of Jesus, that indeed 'without Him, we can do nothing,' then, and only then, will we begin to be genuine people of prayer. Only then will we be people who enjoy a close relationship with God Himself.

We often pray in the flesh, depending on our own wisdom instead of yielding to the Spirit. When we are 'in the flesh,' even in what Miss Bertha Smith[11] called 'religious flesh,' it is a waste of time and effort. The flesh, or old nature, relies upon its own wisdom, human ability and effort. There is a sense of deadness, of drudgery, or boredom in this kind of praying. It is like walking through a mud-filled

---

[10] *Living Water; Studies in John 4*, Martyn Lloyd-Jones.

[11] Bertha Smith served as a missionary in China for many years with the SBC Foreign Mission Board (now called the International Mission Board). She wrote her story in a book called, Go Home and Tell. I was blessed by her ministry and influenced greatly by her teaching.

hole, or a path engulfed in quicksand. It is hard work and spiritually unfulfilling. When *we* are doing the praying, it is like being behind a car while attempting to push it down the road. When we are praying in the Spirit, however, we are inside of the car, riding joyfully along the freeway.

I told a friend of mine recently about an experience I had when I preached a sermon to a local congregation. I had asked several of my 'prayer-warrior' friends to pray for me. As I preached that morning, it felt as though I was swimming in glory, taking backstrokes on a stream that was freely flowing from the throne-room of heaven! Prayer 'in the Spirit' is like riding a wave on a surfboard. There is no effort (if you know how to stay on the board!) The wave is flowing; you are simply letting it carry you along wherever it is going.

Praying 'in the Spirit' is when the Holy Spirit is in control of the prayer. We don't have to be saying anything. We simply allow Him to work through us to accomplish what He wants to do. He is the one who carries our prayers to the throne of heaven, and who imparts the blessing to someone for whom we are praying.

Another thing, about which we need to be warned, is that Satan is very much at work in our lives, trying to keep us from being clean vessels through whom the Spirit can work. Prayer is spiritual warfare, as well as a glorious time to 'ride the wave.' Sometimes prayer is very hard work and the spiritual battle so great, that we become afraid that we might not survive the battle. We must be sure to wear the spiritual armor each day, or we will never be successful in waging a spiritual fight. We need to be alert to the strategies and deceits that our enemy uses on us, but we must be careful to focus on Jesus, not on Satan.

This morning, as I was cooking breakfast, I listened to a radio preacher who was delivering a message about Satan. He made a statement that I have used in Bible classes when teaching on Ephesians 6. (It is in this chapter that Paul wrote about how to wear the spiritual armor needed by Christians each day.) The preacher reminded his church members that we must not take either of two extremes when thinking about Satan and demons. He said, "Some people fall for the lie that Satan does not exist, while others see him and demons 'behind every rock.'" I often warned my students to be aware of Satan's tactics, and to know what the Bible teaches about him. But I reminded them of the necessity to keep our focus on Jesus, who has defeated our enemy. We fight and overcome the powers of darkness when we are properly equipped with the Spirit and the armor of God.

We must be aware that our real battles in life and in prayer are often influenced negatively by Satan and fallen angels. So we must focus on God, His indwelling Spirit, and the promises of God...not on our enemy. Part of Satan's success in defeating Christians, while keeping us from prayer, is to distract us and make us afraid. We must not fall for his tricks anymore. God will deal with him. We must do our best to walk with, obey, and worship our Lord.

Several years ago, a lion escaped from a traveling circus into a small town not far from where I live. I remember hearing about this, and wondered what the people were doing to catch the animal. I am certain that it was a frightening time for them, when they learned about the lion's presence in their community. I remember how I felt when I learned about a large coyote prowling in my neighborhood. I wanted to do everything I could to protect myself and my small pups. It didn't help my panic-level to learn that the coyote had already caught and carried off a small dog!

It will be wise for us to treat Satan as a wild, and even rabid, beast that is loose in the world. His major hatred is toward God. You and I are his favorite targets! How can we ever neglect to wear the entire armor of God daily, being prayer warriors who ask God to protect our lives and the lives of our loved ones?

Peter knew the danger that we Christians face. He wrote about our enemy in his first letter.

> *Be alert and of sober mind. Your enemy the devil prowls around like a roaring lion looking for someone to devour. Resist him, standing firm in the faith, because you know that the family of believers throughout the world is undergoing the same kind of sufferings.*
> (I Peter 5:8-9)

God's Spirit indwells us; He empowers us. He prays through us and for us. He teaches us, guides us, convicts us, and comforts us. We need Him if we want to be successful in waging spiritual warfare, and we need Him if we want to be able to claim God's promises. We cannot experience the abundant life that Jesus wants for us without the Spirit's help. We cannot pray effectively or receive the blessings that God has for us, WITHOUT the Spirit's infilling. What are you doing to keep your life open to God's Spirit and will for your life?

Key 6:

Learn How to Listen to God

I cannot remember when I learned the basic differences between an introvert and an extrovert, but that information has been very helpful to me in many ways, even when it comes to my understanding of prayer. I have come to realize that we need to have basic information about 'what makes us tick', in order to understand how our personality type can affect how we pray. Whether we prefer to talk or to listen... are quick to speak or want to ponder information before we say anything...is information that sheds light on how we can have a more enjoyable and productive relationship with God in prayer. We should think about whether we learn best when we talk, or when we quietly think about something. In times of prayer, do we enjoy talking to God, or would we rather read the Bible and hear God speak while we reflect on what we read? Do we gain more insight about what God may be saying to us when we 'process out loud with someone else', or do we prefer to be alone as we ponder truths from the Bible? Is there a direct correlation between how we relate to humans, and how we communicate with God? Do we relate to Him in the same way we prefer to interact with people?

As I thought more about these issues regarding our personality and our relationship with God in prayer, certain things began to become clear to me ... things that have helped me in my walk with God. I hope that some lessons I have learned will be helpful to you.

How a Person's Basic Personality and Life's Experiences Affect Their Prayers

There is much information on the topic of personality in people. It would take an entire book just to discuss those theories, and how various scholars think personality affects our lives, thoughts, actions, and even how we worship. In this chapter, we will examine a few basic facts to keep in mind, as we think about how to hear from God. Of course, how we relate to Him in various types of prayers (like praise, petition, etc.) can also be affected by our personality type, our personal preferences, and even our past experiences. We cannot go into depth on each of these topics, of course, but I do believe that there are some basic facts that can help us understand how to be more proficient at listening to God.

There are basic differences between Introverts and Extraverts[12] (as viewed by the Myers Briggs Type Inventory) which can influence the ways we 'hear from God.'

According to Myers-Briggs,[13] each of us relates to the world (and to one another) out of our personalities and preferences, some that we were taught, and some that we inherited. Myers and Briggs grouped these differences into four categories. The category that may best address the issue of hearing God is Introversion vs. Extraversion.

---

[12] The spelling that is preferred in the Myers Briggs Type inventories.

[13] Isabel Briggs Myers and Peter Myers, Gifts Differing: Understanding Personality Type (Davies-Black Publishing: Mountain View Calif., 1980. Also see: http://www.myersbriggs.org/my-mbti-personality-type/mbti-basics/

Introvert(I)/Extravert(E)

The descriptors, Introvert and Extravert, actually have little to do with our social approach to others. It has more to do with how we prefer to interact with the world, and how we receive energy. The extravert **(E)** engages others easily; the introvert **(I)** will not open up as quickly. **E's** are energized by being with people - the more the better. Being around too many people for too long a time will drain the **I**, who gains energy by being alone and quiet.

How might these differences affect one's prayer life, especially when seeking to hear from God? The Introvert would probably prefer silence and time to ponder what God might be saying to him/her. The Extravert would probably 'hear' what God might be saying, while actually talking the situation over with someone else. And the Introvert wants time to reflect and worship and pray. The Extravert would rather be in a group of people who are talking about issues. Extraverts prefer prayer meetings where there is a lot of talking going on, while Introverts prefer prayer meetings where there is time for personal reflection and reading of the Scripture.

The study which Myers-Briggs did on personality differences is a good source of information. I recommend that you read it. Each personality trait which they mention can be an influencing factor on how we hear from God. Of course, there are many variables at play, but one helpful thing that we can do (even without knowing all of this information about personality types) is to think about how God has spoken to us in the past. I have found in my own life that there are some primary ways that God speaks to me. But, I also realize that God might decide to speak and lead me by other means, depending on various things occurring in my life at the time.

I will mention some of the basic ways God leads most of us, and later in this chapter, I will give personal examples of how He has led me to recognize His voice. But, in the meantime, it will be helpful to remember this one fact: Myers-Briggs' study on personality types reminds us that we are all different, and God knows how best to speak to each one of us!

Some Basic Principles to Keep in Mind When Attempting to Hear from God

1. God loves to communicate with His children. He is always ready to speak and to listen to us. He is not playing a game of hide-and-seek with us. More than anything, He wants us to hear from Him. So, if we are having difficulty hearing Him, we can be assured that the problem is with us, not with Him. I am convinced that He is talking to us a lot more than we are hearing!

2. God speaks to His children in many different ways that are often determined by us: our needs, our personalities, our faith, our experiences, our willingness to hear and to be led. Ponder just how many ways you try to communicate with your children or with other people, for instance. Much of what you say depends on their age, their disposition at the time, your purpose in speaking to them, etc. I even communicate in different ways with my two pups! So, God is very creative in how He speaks to us. Our job is to be alert and open to His ways and messages.

3. Hearing and understanding how God speaks to us is something that we learn how to do as we walk with Him. This is not always easy, of course. It takes time. We also learn from mistakes, as well as from times when we are successful.

When I was trying to teach my young pups how to do what I wanted them to do, it was necessary to repeat the lesson several times. I rewarded them each time they heard and obeyed me. And now, it is nice when they do what I ask them to do, even without the 'bribe.'

God speaks to us in many ways. He continues to work with us until we learn to do what He wants. And, I am sure that He loves it when we 'finally get the lesson!'

4. God knows the best way to get through to each of us, and a pattern of how He does it will often become obvious to us. I have learned some of the major ways in which God leads me. He speaks clearly to me when I am worshipping while praise music is playing. Somehow, the music opens up a channel between me and Him, allowing His messages to come through to me very clearly. Other ways He speaks to me are: as I read and ponder the Scripture; while reading Christian books; as I listen to others preach or teach. He also speaks to me through inner impressions…a feeling that something is right or wrong for me. I have also experienced His strong voice while I was teaching or preaching, as He put an illustration into my mind to share with the group.

It is important for you to try to notice if there are particular patterns or ways that God speaks to you. This does not mean that He is limited to these ways, of course, but He often uses methods which communicate with how we are 'wired.'

5. Those who know God should be able to hear when He speaks. (John 10: 3-4, 27). Jesus said that His sheep would know and hear His voice… and would follow Him. If we are not experiencing this in our lives, it is urgent for us to check to make sure that we have asked Him into our lives to be our Savior AND our Lord. Jesus will not force His Lordship upon us; but He also will not speak when He knows that we will not obey.

6. We should make a commitment to be a good 'God-listener,' and should actually ask the Lord to speak to us. (I Sam 3:9) The Lord is a gentleman. He will never force Himself upon us. He will convict us if we are out of His will, or if we do not know Him as our Savior and Lord. But He is eager for us to want to listen to Him. He also knows how difficult it is at times to understand what He is saying to us. There is much 'interference on the line' or 'static in the air.' But when we tell Him that we want to hear from Him, He will work to make His messages clear to us.

7. God often does not speak when He knows that we are not willing to do His will, or that we are satisfied NOT to hear from Him. This must break His heart. You know how it feels to want to communicate with someone, and they seem unwilling to listen to you. We absolutely must realize how much our wonderful Lord wants to share His heart and His love with us! When we even begin to realize this truth, we can no longer be satisfied NOT to hear from Him. We will realize that having fellowship with Him is why we were created in the first place!

This is a helpful prayer which you should pray regularly:

"Precious Lord, I want to hear You speak, and I want to do Your will. I realize the sinfulness and rebellion of my own heart, so I choose by faith to listen to You and to obey whatever You say to me. I am willing to be made willing, if my heart and my mind are deceiving me. I give you permission to do whatever it takes to keep me in the center of Your will. Speak, Lord. I am listening."

One of the heart-wrenching questions we must ask ourselves is this: "Do we really want God to speak to us?" All words from God demand an action, a reply of commitment and surrender. God expects a response of love and obedience. Perhaps this is one of the chief reasons why we do not hear more often from God. He has already spoken, and we have not responded.

If we **do** really want to hear from God, and our commitment is to obey what He says, no matter what that is, there are some things that can help us. Take time to read the following passages, and **circle** *the statements that you think are true about your life...some of the criteria for being on 'hearing ground.'* Put an **asterisk** *beside the ones you need to work on.*

1. We must be sure that we are one of His children.
   (John 8:47; 10:3,14)

2. We must be living a life of obedience. (Luke 6:46; James 1:22)

3. We must be cleansed from all known sin and disobedience. (Isa 59:1-2)

4. We must spend time with the Lord daily in worship, Bible study, and prayer. (Acts 1:14, 24; 2:42)

5. We must be responsive to the Spirit's voice and leadership. (John 14:26; Acts 8:29)

6. We must be able to discern the leadership of God when He speaks through circumstances. (Acts 16:6-10)

7. We should be in the habit of humbly asking Him to speak to us. (I Sam 3:10)

8. We must make a rational choice to be a good listener to the voice of God. (Ps. 85:8)

Did you discover some areas where you might improve, in order to be able to hear God speak more clearly? What plans will you make to correct these weaknesses?

Things to Help Us to Discern What God is Saying to Us

We can probably agree that sometimes it is difficult to know what God is saying to us. There are voices and messages from various places that are clamoring to get our attention and to affect our decisions and our behavior. We need all of the help we can get! It is not easy to hear heavenly things while living in a very corrupt world and in a body that has its own will and sinful inclinations. But, there are things that we

CAN and MUST do to help ourselves, as we seek to get better at hearing and obeying God. *Here are a few things to keep in mind:*

1. We need sound theology and doctrinal beliefs. When I was a professor, one of my classes was on cult groups in America. During one semester, when I was teaching the course, I received a call from a local pastor who told me about two of his church members who were being influenced to join a cult. He had talked with them, but was not able to help them see where that particular group was teaching wrong theology. He asked if I would be willing to meet with the couple to try to keep them from making such a huge mistake. I arranged to meet them at the church where I was serving as a bi-vocational Minister of Education. I was not familiar with the cult group that had reached out to the couple, so I spent time reading about them before our meeting. What I did not know until that night, however, was that their cult-recruiter would also be at the meeting. I was thankful I had done my homework!

What was the most helpful to me that night, however, was not my extensive study about the cult's doctrine. The most helpful preparation to deal with the error I would confront was the fact that I was so familiar with Biblical truth, I could easily spot when their teaching disagreed with it. And that was how I helped the church members make their decision. They began to evaluate what they already knew from Scripture with the doctrine presented to them by the cult leaders. Their decisions were now being based on sound theology.

When we know what truth is, we can spot error more easily. When we get an impression that causes us to wonder if it is from God, or from ourselves or Satan, it is easier to determine truth from fiction when we have sound theology.

2. We need to know how to use the Bible, to be able to find answers in it. God knew that we humans would have difficulty discerning His voice. That is one of the chief reasons for His preserving His word through the ages.

Do you ever leave a sticky-note somewhere, or put an event with a reminder alert on your smart phone, as ways to help you remember what to do, or where to be on a certain date? It is helpful to think of the Bible as God's huge sticky-notes to us! We have heard the Bible called 'God's love-letters,' which I think is a wonderful concept. But, I also think it would be helpful for us to view the Bible as being God's 'personal reminders' to us.

Another question: do you ever have so many reminder notes laying around that you don't look at any of them? Let's be careful never to treat the Bible in that way! We need to know how to study it, if we want to be able to clearly understand what God's will is for us.

3. We need prayer and worship... two things that will help us experience 'being still enough' to listen to God. Just this past week, I was talking with a young man who shared with me about his difficulty in knowing what God is saying to him. As we talked, I could see in his eyes that his mind had wandered off somewhere. The 'glassy-eyed stare' happens when we leave a conversation and go somewhere else in our mind. At that moment of wandering, we do not hear what is being said to us. Our minds are preoccupied with what we are thinking. Focusing on what humans are saying takes hard work and focus. The same is true when we want to hear from God. Our minds wander. There are various ways to deal with this, including praying out loud, asking God to help us focus, training our minds to be still, etc. Bible reading and worshipping with music are two helpful ways to keep our minds focused. When we are too 'noisy in our heads,' it is hard to hear God's still, small voice.

4. It is important to have relationship and conversation with Christians who are more mature than we are. Unfortunately, some Christians do not take advantage of the opportunity to learn from others who have walked with the Lord for more years than they have. As a professor, I saw both types of students in my classes: those who were teachable, and those who were not. And this included many who were following a call to some kind of ministry vocation! Some sought out professors with whom they agreed theologically. Others wanted to talk with professors and students who held different theological beliefs, because they wanted to be challenged in their thinking.

One thing is certain: if we ever get to the place that we cannot learn from someone else, it is certain that we have become unteachable...and we are hurting our own spiritual growth! We should read Christian classics in order to learn from those saints of yesteryear, who wrote down the wisdom which they gained from study and experience. And, of course, studying the Bible and learning from the strengths and weaknesses of Biblical characters is a wise practice, if we want to be on 'hearing ground' with God.

5. We need to understand our own abilities, weaknesses, interests, spiritual gifts, etc. I remember the struggle that one of my students had with understanding God's call on his life. He had answered what he felt was a call to preach. He had shared his commitment to the call of God with his home church, and had spent three years in college working toward the goal of being a pastor. One day, after a class (in which we talked about how our calling is something that should bring us great joy and fulfillment), he came by my office to talk. During the course of the conversation, he told me that he was sure God had called him, but he shared that he hated to preach! We talked more, and I suggested that his call might be to serve as a minister of education. (He had shared with me about his love for administration and teaching.) The lightbulb seemed to go on in his head when I mentioned that possibility to him. I heard from him many years later. He had gone to seminary after he finished college, majoring in Religious Education. He shared that he had served in a church as Minister of Education for several years, remarking: "I simply love what I am doing."

God knows how He made us, and how are the most meaningful ways we can serve Him. Many times, our problem is not allowing Him to show us how His will actually fits into who we are. Of course, He may take us out of our comfort zones on occasion, but if He does, He will empower us to do something which we may not have even dreamed was possible for us. Our responsibility is to be good listeners to God, as well as good followers. Part of that 'following' may mean that we don't know all of the answers *when* we want to know them! Sometimes His lack of direction is a way to teach us lessons of faith, while we take daily steps with Him. We probably want the entire plan, in specific detail, to be laid out for us, but He prefers a step-by-step relationship with Himself!

6. Commitment and obedience are essential. Would you tell someone what you wanted them to do, if you already knew that they would not do it? Most of us would save ourselves from that pain. It feels too much like rejection. Could it be that sometimes the Lord does not speak to us, because He knows that we won't do what He says... that we are not really ready to hear Him? As painful as that possibility might be for us to consider, I think it is true. I believe that we sometimes do not hear from God, because we are not willing to do what He says to do, or to stop doing. Commitment to the Lordship of Christ, having the attitude of 'Yes, Sir,' may be the single most important issue of whether we hear from God, or not.

7. We must trust where we cannot understand. Most of us want complete clarity before we venture off to do God's will. Some problem issues and questions that come to mind while I am seeking to hear from God are these: "How will I be able to do what He is asking me to do?" "When will I know the correct time to do something?" "Is this really God, or is it just my own thoughts?" Many of these questions surface when we are seeking to hear God, but they also come after we have heard from Him! We experience self-doubt regarding our ability to follow Him, as well as the fear of not having all of the answers about what the future holds for us. Our main focus should be to learn how to be better listeners, and to trust Him when we don't understand. We should always remember this: we can ask Him for His help in everything!

One of my close friends calls herself an 'army brat,' because her father was a sergeant in the army. She was accustomed to moving frequently, whenever her father received his orders. I used to think that it might be nice to get an envelope from God with my orders, if not every day, at least when big decisions have to be made. But our Father is not that impersonal. We should view the will of God as an adventure WITH Someone who loves us completely, who walks with us, and who will tell us what direction to take when we have to make a decision. Until those forks in the road occur, we should just keep walking with Him and enjoying His companionship. We should be diligent to walk with Him, to obey His leading, and to enjoy His company. The more we do this, the easier it will be. And, we will discover that He has led us even when we did not realize it.

8. We must remember that God has His own timing. It is only so consoling to read the verse, *"With the Lord a day is like a thousand years, and a thousand years are like a day."* (2 Peter 3:8) Thankfully, Peter added some encouraging words to that statement: *"The Lord is not slow in keeping His promise, as some understand slowness. He is patient with you, not wanting anyone to perish, but everyone to come to repentance."* (vs. 9) Although the context of these statements in 2 Peter is about the return of Christ, the truths that Peter shares should give us encouragement when we are waiting to hear from the Lord. God knows when we are ready to hear...and ready to do His will. Sometimes we are the reason that the heavens are silent. We are not ready to obey. At other times, the reason for His silence is because the timing is not right.

9. We must not decide HOW God must speak to us. It is easy to make up some kind of 'fleece' to put out... something for God to do before we will believe that He is speaking to us. We read about Gideon putting out a fleece to be sure of God's leadership...and we think we can do the same thing. Jesus discussed this misconception when He said: "*A wicked and adulterous generation asks for a miraculous sign!*" We don't need a sign. We have the written word of God, as well as the indwelling Holy Spirit, to guide us. It is perilous to make up some kind of sign for God to do before we will believe He has spoken, since both Satan and coincidence can cause things to happen.

Balance in Discerning God's Voice

On Sunday mornings, I listen to Christian music on the radio while I am getting reading to go to church. One difficulty that I run into, however, happens when the weather is rainy. The weather causes a great deal of static on the radio, since the station is located many miles from my home. Sometimes I continue to listen, in spite of the distracting static. On other occasions, I give up! This problem with the static is a good analogy about my effort to 'tune into' the voice of God. Sometimes His voice is very clear. At other times, there is so much 'static', that I give up trying to listen. It is during times like those that I resort to other ways to 'hear Him speak.' In fact, I would recommend to you that there are *three basic ways* to hear God's voice, and to test whether we are hearing correctly. The safest way to be certain we are getting the correct message from God is when all of these three approaches agree. Like a three-legged stool with an uneven leg, our understanding of God's message will not be correct, if we do not use all three of the following tests.

TEST 1: The Word of God

One of the surest ways to hear from God is to read His word. I remember hearing a teacher suggest that often when we ask the Lord to speak to us about something, He will reply: "That answer is pre-recorded." In other words, we really do not have to ask Him about it…the answer is already in the Bible. Reading and studying the Bible is a great way to learn what God wants us to know. It also will help us discern whether some impressions we have, or messages we hear, coincide with what we know to be true about God, as recorded in Scripture. If you know your friend or loved-one very well, you would be the first to speak up for them if someone accused them of saying or doing something that you knew could not be true about them.

It is best to become a student of the Bible if you want to become more proficient at hearing the voice of God. And don't forget to ask the Holy Spirit to teach you every time you read it. That is one of His major roles: to help us to understand truth. (John 16:13) It is helpful to remember these passages, a reminder of the importance of Bible study in your own life.

> *Your word is a lamp for my feet, a light on my path. (Ps. 119:105)*

> *Do your best to present yourself to God as one approved, a worker who does not need to be ashamed and who correctly handles the word of truth. (II Tim.2:15)*

All Scripture is God-breathed and is useful for teaching, rebuking, correcting and training in righteousness, so that the servant of God may be thoroughly equipped for every good work.(2 Tim.3:16)

TEST 2: Outer Circumstances

Another important way to understand what God is saying to us is learning how to discern His leadership when He uses things like: opened and closed doors, our personal abilities and talents, other people, and our own common sense. God does expect us to use the brains that He gave to us; to learn how to watch what He is doing in the world; to discern the meaning of a closed or opened door of opportunity; to reason what is best from a human standpoint, etc. Examining these things should not be the ONLY way we understand God's leading, but they are certainly important ones. I have found that it is also good to see if there is a pattern to the usual way the Lord leads me. I have discovered through the years that, on many occasions, when He wants me to take a different pathway, He makes me dissatisfied with where I am. I was a professor for 30 years before I began to be dissatisfied with what I was doing. It was His way of leading me to leave that assignment, and to take one at our local Baptist Association. He has used the same pattern a number of times in my life, as I sought to know His will about something.

The lot is cast into the lap, but the decision is wholly of the Lord [even the events that seem accidental are really ordered by Him].
(Prov. 16:33, Amp. Version)

But I will stay on at Ephesus until Pentecost, because a great door for effective work has opened to me, and there are many who oppose me. (I Cor. 16:8-9)

Now when I went to Troas to preach the gospel of Christ and found that the Lord had opened a door for me. (2 Cor. 2:12)

TEST 3: Inner Impressions

Another important method of discerning God's voice is to listen to the inner impressions of our heart and mind. This test is difficult to describe, but it is imperative that we learn how to discern inner impressions. Some have described these impressions as a 'gut feeling.' Or they say that they 'just knew.' That is only so helpful when you are trying to explain to someone else how you felt or heard a message from God.

When I was in my final year of doctoral studies at Southwestern Seminary, I sent out a resume to every Baptist College and University in the country, since I had felt a call from God to teach. Many months went by before I heard anything from any of them. That silence alone produced a great deal of anxiety in me, since my school would not confer a doctorate if the candidate did not have a job! Finally, I received two invitations from universities to come for a visit to interview for a teaching position. The crisis occurred, however, when I could not get peace about accepting a position at either of them! I struggled tremendously, trying to get an answer from the Lord. Peace came when I said 'no' to both schools.

It made no rational sense for me to turn these jobs down. Nothing in the Bible would lead me to say 'No.' I had been called to do the very thing that the schools were offering me the opportunity to do. It was this third 'test' that finally helped me to make a decision. It is always best NOT to do something if you do not have peace about it. You may have fear or confusion, or even excitement about an offer; but if you do not have peace about the decision, you need to either pray more, or say "No." A verse in the book of Colossians speaks directly to this issue:

> *And let the peace (soul harmony which comes) from Christ rule (act as umpire continually) in your hearts [deciding and settling with finality all questions that arise in your minds, in that peaceful state] to which as [members of Christ's] one body you were also called [to live]. And be thankful (appreciative), [giving praise to God always]. (Col. 3:15, Amp. N.T.)*

It will also be helpful for you to study these passages:

> *Roll your works upon the Lord [commit and trust them wholly to Him; He will cause your thoughts to become agreeable to His will, and] so shall your plans be established and succeed.*
> *(Prov. 16:3, Amp. N.T.)*

And your ears will hear a word behind you, saying, This is the way; walk in it, when you turn to the right hand and when you turn to the left. (Isa. 30:21, Amp. N.T.)

Paul and his companions traveled throughout the region of Phrygia and Galatia, having been kept by the Holy Spirit from preaching the word in the province of Asia. ⁷ When they came to the border of Mysia, they tried to enter Bithynia, but the Spirit of Jesus would not allow them to. (Acts 16:6-7)

WARNINGS:

1. **God is not the only one who speaks to humans**. The devil is also speaking; trying to keep us away from the will and purposes of God. There are several methods that he uses to speak to us, one of which is by disguising himself as an 'angel of light,' or as the Holy Spirit. He whispers into our minds and hearts, and even works in circumstances. He also speaks through the lips of other people. He is a master at twisting the Bible. Do you remember how he twisted it when tempting Jesus in the wilderness experience? (Matt. 4) Because of these and other deceptive methods, it is ALWAYS wise for you to confirm your impressions in discussion with another believer. This can help you determine whether or not it is truly God who is speaking to you. You should be cautious, however, being sure that the person you ask for feedback and confirmation is someone who is walking with the Lord. And, of course, you should

always evaluate your impressions by what the Bible teaches.

2. **Do not always believe it to be true when someone says that God has spoken to him/her, especially if they are trying to persuade you to do something.** Whenever that happens, you should always say to God, "Lord, confirm it in my heart and spirit, and through Your Word." Do not be led astray by well-meaning people. It is easy to be confused by people who THINK that their own thoughts are God's voice. Quite frequently at the university where I taught, co-eds would share with me that they were having doubts about whether or not they should date a certain person. They sometimes told me that the person in question had assured her that he had received a message from God about her being the person he was to marry. I would always advise her to ask God to confirm that message to her heart, and that she needed to realize how difficult it is to be objective in situations like that! I also reminded her of the value of the opinions of family and friends who knew both people.

If Satan sometimes 'imitates God,' how can we know whether an impression is from God, or when it is from the devil? That question is a tough one, but one of the best ways is to learn what the Bible teaches about how God and Satan usually speak and work! Complicating this whole issue is the fact that we have our own opinions and 'voices' inside of our head, clamoring to be heard! Are there any tips to clarify all of this confusion? I can remember wondering these very things when I was a student in seminary, many years ago. My pastor recommended a booklet to me by Martin Knapp, entitled <u>Discerning Impressions</u>, published by Christian Publications in Northridge, Ca. I have been unable to locate the book since then, but I kept some of the information from it. I have found his tips to be very helpful as I try to discern the differences between what may be God's voice, what are merely my own desires, or when Satan is attempting to influence me. I hope this information will be helpful to you.

When God Gives Us Impressions

The Holy Spirit works in our hearts and minds to help guide us along God's paths. According to Knapp, all impressions from God bear four distinguishing features:

1. Scriptural: in harmony with God's will as revealed in His Word.

The Spirit will never impress us to go against God's word. It doesn't matter how many ways we might rationalize an impression, or try to reason that Bible truths from the past do not fit today's culture, we are in trouble if we ever go against what is clearly taught in God's word. Of course, I realize that sometimes there are differences of opinion about what the Bible is actually saying. In those instances, we should ask the Lord to show us clearly if our impressions are from Him. He wants us to know and to do His will, so when we choose to do His will, no matter how difficult it may seem, He will move heaven and earth to make sure that we understand what He wants. Many times, our confusion comes because we are not willing to do what He impresses us to do...or we are afraid of what the ramifications will be if we obey what we are sensing is the right thing to do.

2. Right: in harmony with God's will as revealed in man's moral nature (the rule of right and wrong).

I remember learning about an indigenous tribe in rural Brazil that had an unusual code of ethics. The women were naked from the waist up, except for a necklace of beads. Some traders discovered the tribe, and tried to entice the women to trade their beads for certain commodities. If any of the women decided to make the trade, they would go behind a tree, take off their necklace and hand it around the tree to the trader. They did not want the person to see them naked!

There are 'moral codes' everywhere. We adopt a system of right and wrong from the family and society into which we were born. Although the 'rule of right and wrong' might be vastly different in various cultures, God has placed morality into the heart of man. When we hear a voice telling us to depart from our moral beliefs (unless we have grown to understand that our original standard is not Biblical), we can be sure that it is NOT an impression from the Spirit. Hopefully, our value system has been influenced by godly people.

3. Providential: in harmony with God's will as revealed in providential dealings (opened and closed doors).

The apostle Paul often used this method to determine what God wanted him to do, or where he was to go on his next mission adventure. As he traveled through Phrygia and Galatia (Acts 16:6), he was actually *'kept by the Holy Spirit from preaching the word in the province of Asia.'* This was a closed door. Paul was sensitive to the possible reason: the Spirit had another place for him to go. Perhaps another location would be more fruitful. Perhaps the Spirit was protecting Paul from harm. Whatever the reason for this closed door may have been, Paul did not attempt to open it on his own. Unfortunately, at times, many of us try to push through a closed door anyway! And we can also fail to go through a door that the Lord has opened for us.

4. Reasonable: in harmony with God's will as revealed to spiritually enlightened judgment (sanctified common sense).

Note the word 'sanctified' before 'common sense.' God does expect us to use the brains that he gave us, to reason out what we think we might be hearing from God. But common sense must be 'sanctified'... thinking and reasoning that is guided by past experience with God, knowledge of His will, and commitment to Him. Sometimes, He may speak what seems to be completely irrational to the unsanctified mind. For instance, did it make sense for Abraham to feel impressed to sacrifice his only son? It made no sense to kill the one whom God promised would be the channel through which He would bless the nations. But Abraham knew God to be Someone who could, and would, redeem something which seemed totally irrational. He knew that God could raise Isaac from the dead, if Abraham killed him. His thinking/common sense was controlled and influenced by what he knew and believed about God. And so must ours be.

What do the Inner 'Voices' sound like?

It is not easy to tell who is speaking to us, whether the 'voices' are our own thoughts, or if they come from Satan. Knapp also shared some helpful tips that can help us be clear about what we are 'hearing.'

1. When God speaks, he does not yell at us or tell us to hurry. He doesn't ever say that if we don't do something immediately, He will not speak again. He gives us time to pray, and to ask Him for clarification. He leads; He does not push. Of course, there are times when God speaks, and it sounds loud to us, especially if we are pushing against His will in any way. The best thing to do is to tell Him that you want to do His will, and that you WILL do it, when He makes it clear to you. You can share your fears and worries with Him, and ask Him to take care of those things/people that are your concern if you do follow His will.

2. Impressions from God will grow over time. You should always walk in the direction that you think is God's will for you, while asking Him to open or close the right doors to clarify your impressions. What is urgent to remember is that God's will is always best for us. We can choose it even when we are not clear what it is!

3. God's impressions always 'welcome the light.' In other words, we can talk with people about our impressions, checking with mature Christians about what we think we are hearing from God. Suggestions from Satan, as well as those from ourselves, many times are ones that we do not want to share with others. We must be careful from whom we ask advice, however, because we can always find someone who will agree with anything we share with them!

4. If there is great fear or guilt in what you are hearing, you can be sure that those impressions are either from Satan or from yourself. God never uses guilt to get us to understand, or to do His will. He convicts us when we sin, of course, but His convictions are what I call a 'clean cut.' He does not harass us or make us feel ashamed. He points out the problem and the sin, and then reminds us that He is willing to forgive us when we ask Him to do so.

5. *If there are threats about what will happen to you or to your family if you do not do what the impression is telling you to do, you can be assured that this message is not from God.* Satan loves to speak loudly, to harass and make us feel guilty. He loves to make us afraid, to tell us that we are unworthy of God, or that we have already waited too long to do what God wants. He makes us feel ashamed and afraid. He reminds us of our sins. When we do not listen to or obey his impressions, they will grow dim. The will of God will remain in our thoughts, and will grow stronger. God will continue to speak in a low, tender, still and soft voice. He will assure us of His love, His protection, His guidance, and His companionship. And as we walk in the direction that we feel God is leading, our conviction that we have heard from God will grow stronger.

It is so important to fill our minds with what is written in the Word of God. We learn about Him…what He is like. We learn how He spoke to others. We understand His will, as recorded in these sacred pages. All of these truths will serve as a powerful test when we have any impression. We should always ask ourselves when we hear an impression: (1) Did God ever act that way or speak that way in the Bible to any of His other children? (2) Is that the way God works? (3) Are there any promises in the Bible against which I can test my impressions? The word of God is such a valuable source in so many ways. And it certainly is an important one when it comes to discerning the many voices that resound in our minds!

Pitfalls to Avoid

There are common mistakes that we humans make when trying to discern what God might be saying to us. Here are a few for you to be on guard against:

1. Relying too heavily on feelings. Since impressions often seem to be like feelings, it is easy for us to be confused. When we feel God's peace or joy, or even human happiness, it is very easy for us to conclude that God is speaking, because we feel happy, or that He is not speaking, because we feel depressed. This is not true. God's voice is deeper than emotions. This is one reason why we must rely on all three 'tests' when we are trying to discern what God is saying to us. God's word and other circumstances must agree with what we are feeling. Those 'tests' are a reality check on our emotions. Since many psychologists say that feelings only last 8-30 seconds unless we 'feed them' with a thought, it is best to allow some time to pass before we act on most impressions.

2. Chance Bible texts. Sometimes, in our zeal to know God's will about something, we try to make God work according to our plans. Even though we know that He speaks through the scriptures, it is dangerous to try to orchestrate that. I have known of some people who would ask the Lord to speak to them while they opened the Bible at random, putting their finger on a verse. Someone jokingly said that we might get into trouble if the verse says, "And he went out and hanged himself!" God does use His word to speak to us, but using a random approach is not a wise way to hear from Him.

3. Imagination: ideas and impressions that we paint in our own minds. It is so easy for us to desire something so much that we talk ourselves into believing that it is the will of God. We can imagine ourselves with a particular person, or doing a particular ministry or job, and we want it so much, that it 'feels so right.' This is one reason why we must talk with mature Christians, those who know us and will help us to be objective. I had many occasions to talk with students who were following what they perceived to be a call to pastor a church. They wanted this dream to be God's will, so they failed to see that they were better equipped for another area of service.

4. Dreams: not God's usual way. We have the Holy Spirit indwelling us. Biblical characters did not. Because there are so many different reasons for dreams, it is wise not to put a great deal of emphasis on them when trying to hear messages from God. Of course, if God wants to speak to us in that way, I believe that He will also confirm the impressions in other ways. Recurring dreams can give us tips about what is going on in our minds. There is value in examining dreams, but there are more reliable ways to hear God speak.

5. Infatuation: something is so enticing that even evil can seem OK, because our 'flesh' wants it. Objectivity is almost impossible when we have a strong desire for something to be God's will. The safest way to deal with these strong desires is by knowing the word of God, and being open to wise counsel from those who know the Lord, and who know us. We must be careful not to rationalize our desires, or to fail to listen to the input of others.

6. Impulse: God never hurries people to do doubtful things (Luke 22:47-51). God gives us time to be sure of His message to us. His voice will become clearer as we continue to pray and seek Him. One key, of course, is to be willing to do what He wants, no matter what that is. We will not get clarity if we are simply seeking His approval for what WE want to do!

7. Passion: stubbornness or righteous indignation; anger. (James 1:19-20) When our emotions are inflamed, it is difficult to be objective or silent enough to hear God speak. We must wait until these strong emotions subside, before we can expect to have clarity on our impressions. And this may take some time.

8. Prejudices and preconceived ideas. (Gal. 2:11-14) If a woman has been raised to think it is wrong for a woman to be a preacher or a deacon, it will be more difficult for her to believe that a call she is sensing might be to pastoral ministry. In a similar way, if a male has the same opinion about gender roles in ministry, he will probably have a difficult time understanding and accepting his wife's calling. When such preconceived ideas involve the theology that we were taught, and are not simply based on tradition, it can be doubly difficult to discern God's will.

9. Opinions of others rather than our own impressions (I Kings 13). But we DO need to be open when God does want to speak to us through others. (Prov. 11:14) Sometimes God will confirm our impressions through others, and at other times, we are the only one who knows what God has said to us. It is hard to go against others. However, if we have tested our impressions, have prayed and sought God, and have waited and studied God's word for clarification, then we must follow what we think and feel is God's will, whether anyone else believes us or not.

10. Signs: 'putting out a fleece' to confirm God's will is immature and loaded with dangers. (Matt. 12:38-40) God can speak through such circumstances, but so can 'chance' and Satan. Many times, the reason we resort to this way of hearing from God may be simply because we do not want to wait for Him to speak or to do something. We feel that we must know, NOW. Or we do not want to go to the trouble to do the other, safer methods of discovering what He is saying to us. Sometimes, we might put out a fleece, and what we have asked to happen, DOES. We then might wonder if what occurred was only chance...so we ask for something else to happen. Believing a fleece takes as much faith as simply asking, and having faith that God will answer in His way, and in His time.

Other Things to Keep in Mind When Seeking to Hear God's Voice

It is interesting to me just how difficult it is to discern God's voice at times, while at other times, there seems to be no doubt about what I am hearing from Him. Perhaps one of the major reasons is that we are still very much tuned into and controlled by our old natures. And there is so much 'noise' in the world, static that keeps us from being able to tune in to the still, quiet voice of God. We need to remember, however, that we can be very certain about God's desire to communicate with us. Fellowship with us is why He created us in the first place!

Because He wants to speak to us, here are a few additional things that can be of help to you in growing closer to Him, and becoming more aware of His presence:

1. Be obedient and responsive to His leading and conviction. It is easy to forget that sin separates us from intimate fellowship with the Father. He is holy; we are not. But we can, and should, be conscientious about keeping our sins confessed and cleansed. God's Spirit is faithful to show us where we have wandered out of God's will, either by accident or quite deliberately. Our responsibility is to ask for, and claim, His forgiveness. He will bless us when we do this. And His voice will be more easily discerned by us.

2. Spend time in reading and studying the Bible, asking for Him to speak to your heart. One of the reasons that the Holy Spirit was given to us is to lead us unto all truth. He is our teacher and guide. Every time we open God's word, we should ask the Spirit to speak truth to us, as we read it. The Bible has been given to us for many reasons, one of which is to let us know what God wants to say to us. He knew that we would sometimes have trouble hearing His voice; so he preserved the written word to help us. It is strategic that His Word be a prominent part of our daily lives.

3. Spend time in worship every day. Worship and praise open up the doorway to the heart of God. Our natural focus is upon ourselves. Praise helps us change that focus to God. Much of the world's appeal and allurement is lost when we spend time in the presence of God via worship. We can more readily understand God's perspective on life, and on what is truly important, when we lift our minds and hearts toward Him. I have found that He speaks most freely to me when I use music to help me worship Him. I have even received an entire sermon from Him as I worshipped! Of course, He uses the written word of God to speak to me each day. But I love the messages that I get from Him when I am enjoying His presence while worshipping!

4. Spend time in silent listening. You will notice just how 'noisy' you are in your mind when you attempt to sit still and listen to God. Really listening to anyone is hard work, and that seems to be doubly true when we try to hear from God. I find that reading the Bible, singing, worshipping, and praying... all help me to be more prepared to listen to God. A quiet, peaceful mind and heart takes preparation. Times at the beach or in the mountains can also quiet your heart, helping you to be more receptive to His voice. And even while reading the Bible, you can ask the Spirit to calm your heart, and help you to hear God speak through His word.

5. If you must make a decision of some kind, it is helpful to list the pros and cons of each decision, and ask Him to 'tip the scale' as you pray. This may take time, as usually there are legitimate reasons why each decision is beneficial. But as you continue to pray and to listen for His voice, you will begin to feel that one of the decisions you have selected is the right one. You should also remember that the sheer number of reasons supporting a decision should not automatically be the deciding factor. What you are waiting for is the peace/impression that a certain decision is the one that God wants you to make.

6. Walk in the direction in which you think He is leading, and ask Him to either trouble you, or to give you peace. Sometimes, it is difficult to know which way is best, which decision is wisest. Start walking toward the decision that you believe is the best one, and give God permission to stop you, to close or open a door according to His will. Tell Him that you choose by faith to do His will, and that you give Him permission to do what it takes to keep you from making the wrong decision.

Whenever I gave this advice to students, some would gasp in fear. "What might He do to me, Dr. C, if I give Him that kind of permission?" I told them that our fear actually said more about us than about God. "I would rather have a broken leg, and be in the center of His will, than have a healthy one and be outside of His will," I would answer.

We must have peace, so when you don't, stay put. Don't make a decision when you don't have peace. Pray until you do. Perhaps you should consider that the alternate decision that you were considering is the correct one after all.

7. Be open to the advice and suggestions of others who walk with God. Be careful about your choice of advisors, however. And always ask God to confirm their counsel, and your impressions by (1) His Word, (2) peace in your heart, and (3) open and closed doors. We can help each other discern God's voice, by praying for each other, and giving good advice, when we feel led by God to do so. The final decision, however, must be yours. Even if someone tells you that they know God's will for you, or that they have a message from God for you, be sure to ask God to affirm it in your own heart.

8. God does expect you to use your mind, if it is dedicated to Him. That is why it is good to think a great deal about decisions, about impressions or feelings that you have. It is best to look at things rationally, and to weigh the positive and negative ramifications. But our minds must be under the Spirit's control. We can, and should, ask God to be Lord of our thinking...to help us to see when something is logical or not. And, we must also realize that when He speaks, sometimes we may not fully understand what He is saying, or what the ramifications might be. Give Him time to clarify all of that for you. It is obviously easier to look back and see how God's leadership makes sense, than it is to understand what He is presently telling us to do.

9. Remember that there are two major enemies who do not want us listening to God: Satan and Self. We will take a look at both of these obstacles:

a) Satan hates God, and because we belong to God, He hates us, also. He hates that God has rescued us from hell, and he wants to disrupt our relationship with God. He wants to hurt God, and to hurt us. He wants to keep us miserable, and he wants to keep us from being of any use in the kingdom of God. Until we realize this about Satan, we will continue to fall for his deceits. He especially hates it when a child of God begins to grasp the power of prayer. We must be alert for his attacks. We must wear the entire armor of God, if we want to be successful in our walk with God.

(b) Self, or the old nature, has one major goal: to be god of our life. Unfortunately, even when we become a Christian, our old nature still is alive and well. The only difference between a Christian and a non-Christian (as far as the old nature is concerned) is that Christians also have a new nature, one that is born of God, and wants to do the will of God. Paul wrote about these two natures in many of his letters. He gave his own testimony in Romans 7 of the struggle that he himself faced; the constant turmoil between his old nature and his new nature. But he also wrote many words of wisdom about how this old nature can be defeated. We must be certain that we understand his teachings on this topic. Many Christians try to reform the old nature, to make it do religious things as they attempt to become more 'spiritual.' But, that is impossible. When Paul wrote, "I die daily,' he was referring to the fact that we have to make a daily choice about which 'nature' we will allow to be in control that day. (Two authors who explain in great detail how to be successful in this battle are Watchman Nee and Andrew Murray.[14] I highly recommend their books to help you become more aware of these two natures, and how to deal with them.)

---

[14] Some of their works that have been a blessing to me are: The Normal Christian Life, and Release of the Spirit by Watchman Nee; and Absolute Surrender, Abide in Christ, and True Vine by Andrew Murray.

When God speaks, things happen. Things come into being. People are transformed... when God speaks. He spoke the world into existence. (Gen.1:3) He spoke to and through prophets. (Heb.1:1-2) He spoke to and through His Son. (Mt. 3:17) He spoke from heaven, and through dreams and visions. He spoke to kings and to the common people. He spoke and gave the Ten Commandments to Moses. He spoke from the heavens, and speaks from within His children.

He spoke about, spoke to, and speaks through His Son. He speaks through the Spirit, and the Spirit offers our prayers back to Him. He wants to have fellowship with us, His children. His desire is to share His love and encouragement and guidance with us, and to crown us with unfathomable blessings. We need to listen, and to walk with our loving Heavenly Father. There is no greater blessing. There is nothing else that can bless the Father's heart.

Conclusion

Many of us have a love-hate relationship with our keys. We hate them at times, because it takes so many of them to be able to access all of the doors, drawers, lock-boxes, storage buildings, etc. that are a part of our daily lives. And we hate it when we need our keys, but cannot locate them. We hate it when they do not work anymore, either because the lock has been changed, or the key has been damaged. We hate it when we have to replace one, especially if it is an electronic key or fob that is very costly. But as much as we might hate our keys, we love it when they give us access to whatever we need or want.

Imagine that you have been to the grocery store, and are now pulling into your driveway. You manage to gather up all of the bags of groceries, and you hang a bag on each of your fingers. You are trying to avoid having to make more than one trip from the car to the house. You walk up to the door, only to discover that your keys are not in either hand. You don't know if you dropped them, or locked them in the car. Your feelings of anger and frustration rise, as you try to decide what to do next. You walk back out to the car, with the packages still hanging from your fingers. You do not find the keys inside of your car, nor are they on the driveway or ground. Your fingers are now giving you a lot of pain, and your mind is flooded with thoughts about how you can solve this dilemma. You reluctantly put the bags on the ground, and search your pockets for the keys. They are not there. You look in the bags, one by one, and finally find the keys in one of the bags. You surmise that they must have fallen out of your hand into the bag. So, you pick up the groceries again, meticulously slipping each plastic bag over a thumb or finger; and you head back to the house. Then you realize that you cannot open the door with the key, because both of your hands have plastic bags hanging from each finger. You place a couple of the bags on the steps, unlock the door, pick up the groceries, and enter your home. But, you fail to turn off the security alarm, so it begins to sound loudly...and your dogs begin to howl.

After the 'crisis' is over, you head for your lounge chair to try to gain your composure. The bags of groceries are sitting in piles on the dining room table. The phone rings. You ignore it. You are too busy trying to figure out how to avoid a rerun of what you have just experienced. You wonder how something as simple as misplaced keys could lead to such a disruption in an otherwise normal day.

Some of us might bring similar frustration upon ourselves when we misplace our 'keys to prayer.' Life has a way of overloading us. We are on our own 'mission' toward finding happiness, relaxation, rewarding interpersonal relationships, and success. But frustration and anger arise when we encounter barriers or other problems that hinder our goals. We are locked out of where we want to be. We don't know what to do. And it does not help us to realize that a lot of other people are also locked out of their dreams.

What can we do? We must realize how urgent it is to know how to find and use the keys that God has provided for us. This is the only way to find true happiness... to unlock the power of prayer. It is in that close relationship with God that we can experience life that is truly worth living. "Enter in to the joy and presence of your Lord, my child," says our loving heavenly Father to each of His children. "We can handle life together."

Appendix Materials

Spiritual Inventory 181

God's Promises and How to Claim Them 189

Testimonies about Prayer 197

Traveling On My Knees

Last night I took a journey
To a land across the seas.
I didn't go by ship or plane
I traveled on my knees.

I saw so many people there
In bondage to their sin,
And Jesus told me I should go,
That there were souls to win.

But I said "Jesus, I can't go
To lands across the seas."
He answered quickly, "Yes, you can
By traveling on your knees."

He said, "You pray, I'll meet the need.
You call, and I will hear.
It's up to you to be concerned
For lost souls far and near."

And so I did; knelt in prayer,
Gave up some hours of ease,
And with the Savior by my side,
I traveled on my knees.

As I prayed on, I saw souls saved
And twisted persons healed,
I saw God's workers strength renewed
While laboring in the field.

I said, "Yes Lord, I'll take the job.
Your heart I want to please.
I'll heed Your call and swiftly go
By traveling on my knees."

Written by Sandra Goodwin

Spiritual Inventory

I. Read the following Scriptures prayerfully and ask the Lord to speak a special message to your heart. When we allow the Spirit to search our hearts, it is an experience that brings us pain at first. We begin to get a glimpse of how we have grieved our Lord. But when we persist with the confession and cleansing, we will experience a peace and joy that have eluded us. And our relationship with the Lord will be a blessed, sweet one.

1. Psalm 139:23-24
2. Isaiah 59:1-3
3. Psalm 51:10-13
4. I John 1:6-10

II. Read the following information slowly and prayerfully, asking the Lord to convict you of any way you have grieved the Spirit. As you are convicted, spend time in prayer confessing your sin and claiming his forgiveness.

Grieve not the Holy Spirit of God, whereby ye are sealed unto the day of redemption. – Eph. 4:30.

"Grieve" is a love word. You cannot grieve someone who does not love you. You can hurt him or anger him, but you cannot grieve him. The Holy Spirit is a loving, tender, sensitive personality. To grieve Him means that we are causing pain to someone who loves us. How can we know what grieves Him? By His names which indicate His nature.

He is the Spirit of truth, so anything false, deceitful, hypocritical, grieves Him.

He is the spirit of faith; so doubt, unbelief, distrust, worry, anxiety, grieve Him. Do you doubt his Word? Is there unbelief regarding the fundamental truths of salvation? Do you worry over your business, your children, your health? If so, you are grieving the Spirit of faith, and He cannot fill you.

He is the Spirit of Grace, so anything which is hard, bitter, ungracious, unthankful, malicious, unforgiving… grieves Him. Is there anybody you will not forgive or to whom you will not speak? Is there someone with whom you have quarreled? Is there bitterness in your heart toward God? Do you spend your days grumbling about your circumstances? Then do not pray to be filled with the Spirit, unless you are willing to be cleansed.

He is the Spirit of holiness, so anything defiling grieves Him. Do you harbor unclean thoughts? Do you read unhealthy books? Do you listen to dirty stories? If so, you are grieving Him.

He is the Spirit of wisdom,…so ignorance, conceit, arrogance and folly grieve Him. The Holy Spirit stands ready to teach us and to reveal the deep things of the Word to us. Our ignorance of the Bible, our pride in our own knowledge and ability, grieve Him. Our failure to read and study God's word breaks His heart.

He is the Spirit of power, love and discipline… so our weakness, fruitlessness, disorderliness and lack of control grieve Him. There are thousands of people all around you who are still unsaved and do not know the Gospel. Perhaps some are in your family. Why can't Christ win them? Perhaps it is because the channels through whom His power should flow are choked with sin. Are you embittered because you have been wronged, and is your life poisoned by unforgiveness or hatred? Do you give way to your bodily appetites, your fleshly desires and your temperamental weaknesses? Failure to spend time in prayer every day grieves Him. When we spend more time asking for blessings than we do in praising, thanking Him or confessing our sins, it grieves Him.

He is the Spirit of Life, so any trace of indifference or apathy grieves Him. Do you go for days without opening your Bible? Do you forget to talk with Him in prayer? Do you attend church out of obligation or routine?

He is the Spirit of glory, so whatever is worldly, earthly, or fleshly grieves Him. Do you love possessions and money more than Him? Do you faithfully give your tithes willingly and cheerfully?

If we willfully allow anything contrary to the Holy Spirit to remain in our lives, it means that we love sin more than we love Him. Such unfaithfulness grieves Him.

HE MUST HAVE CLEAN VESSELS

Spirituality depends upon a harmonious relationship with the indwelling Holy Spirit. When we indulge in known sin, it means that we are living with a grieved Spirit. To be filled, one must be cleansed. God does not require golden vessels, neither does He seek for silver ones, but He must have clean ones.

We grieve the Spirit when we say 'Yes' to Satan and allow him to lure us into sin or disobedience. We quench the Spirit when we say 'No' to God when He woos us into commitment and service.

To bring the believer wholly into the will of God is perhaps the Holy Spirit's hardest task. Self-will is in every one of us and is always bursting out into rebellion. The only cure for it is to have one's heart firmly fixed upon doing God's will as the rule for daily living.

GOD CAN SPOT A COUNTERFEIT

In a darkened room, much dirt can pass unnoticed. But when the doors and windows are opened and the sun shines in, even the dust is revealed. The Holy Spirit brings the sin in our lives out into the light. The more completely He fills us, the more perfect will be the revelation and recognition of sin. The nearer God is to us, the more sensitive to sin we become. Some things, which a year ago you would not have called sin, you now acknowledge for what they are.

God will accept no substitute for confession, and He instantly detects a counterfeit. Have you ever thought that God would accept from you a larger gift of money, greater activity in service or a longer prayer in place of a confession of sin? Many times a confession is but a partial one. Some top sin is mentioned while the root sin is altogether unconfessed. God does not excuse our sin, even when we try to explain it away or take comfort in our human weaknesses.

Some sins need to be confessed only to God, because against Him only have we sinned. Other sins need to be confessed to individuals against whom we have sinned; and a public confession of sin is sometimes necessary when the whole company of God's people have been wronged.

THE SEPARATION THAT HE REQUIRES

The cleansing must be from all defilement of both flesh and spirit. Separation from every defiling thing is God's requirement. God demands a cleansing that reaches from the innermost desire to the outermost deed, that goes from the core to the circumference of our lives.

Time for a "Spiritual Checkup"

The following are some of the features and manifestations of the self-life. The Holy Spirit alone can interpret and apply this to your individual case. As you read, examine yourself in the very presence of God. Underline the phrases or statements God convicts you of, in order to confess them and ask for His forgiveness.

Are you ever conscious of:

A secret spirit of pride--an exalted feeling, in view of your success or position; because of your good training or appearance; because of your natural gifts and abilities; an important, independent spirit?

Love of human praise; a secret fondness to be noticed; love of supremacy, drawing attention to self in conversation; a swelling out of self when you have had a free time in speaking or praying?

The stirrings of anger or impatience, which, worst of all, you call nervousness or holy indignation; a touchy, sensitive spirit; a disposition to resent and retaliate when disapproved of or contradicted; a desire to throw sharp, heated barbs at another person?

Self-will; a stubborn, unteachable spirit; an arguing, talkative spirit; harsh, sarcastic expressions; an unyielding, headstrong disposition; a driving, commanding spirit; a disposition to criticize and pick flaws when set aside and unnoticed; a peevish, fretful spirit; a disposition that loves to be coaxed and humored?

Carnal fear; a man-fearing spirit; a shrinking from reproach and duty; reasoning around your cross; a fearfulness that someone will offend and drive some prominent person away; a compromising spirit?

A jealous disposition, a secret spirit of envy shut up in your heart; an unpleasant sensation in view of the great prosperity and success of another; a disposition to speak of the faults and failings rather than the gifts and virtues of those more talented and appreciated than yourself?

A dishonest, deceitful disposition; the evading and covering of the truth; the covering up of your real faults; leaving a better impression of yourself than is strictly true; false humility; exaggeration; straining the truth?

Unbelief; a spirit of discouragement in times of pressure and opposition; lack of quietness and confidence in God; lack of faith and trust in God; a disposition to worry and complain in the midst of pain, poverty, or at what God is allowing to happen to you and/or your loved ones; an overanxious feeling whether everything will come out all right?

Formality and deadness; lack of concern for lost souls; dryness and indifference; lack of power with God? Prayerlessness? Lack of enthusiasm?

Selfishness; love of ease; love of material possessions and money?

These are only some of the traits which generally indicate a carnal heart. By prayer, hold your heart open to the searchlight of God. *"Search me O God, and know my heart: try me, and know my thoughts: and see if there be any wicked way in me."* (Psalm 139:23,24)

The Holy Spirit will enable you, by confession and faith, to bring your "self-life" to a time of death. Do not minimize your failures, but go to the bottom of the depth of sinfulness and disobedience, and confess it to God. Then you can accept the wonderful cleansing and forgiveness that He has promised.

III. Read the following Scriptures to make sure that you are not overlooking any sin in your life. Ask forgiveness for all of them that the Spirit brings to your mind. Continue confessing and claiming forgiveness until you can honestly say that you know of nothing else you are omitting. Spend time thanking Him for cleansing. Make a list of people with whom you need to talk, confess to, or apologize to, and make every effort to do so this week. Cleansing is not complete until we have been obedient in this matter.

1. Matthew 5:21-28
2. Mark 7:20-23; Mark 11:25-26
3. Galatians 5:19-21, 26
4. Ephesians 4:25-32
5. James 1:26; James 4:2-4
6. Proverbs 16:5, 18; Proverbs 11:13

IV. If you have been earnest and sincere up to this point, you are now ready to present yourself anew to the Lord for His use and glory. Make a list of people and things, situations and concerns which you need to commit to the Lord. Spend time in prayer committing to the Lord everything you are, have desire, etc., such as your mind, body, time, talents, possessions, friends, family, vocation, life's mate, etc. Last of all, surrender yourself. Give God permission to do anything He wants to with you and with all that concerns you. Give up once and for all your <u>right to yourself.</u> By faith make Him Lord of your life in every area.

Read the following Scripture verses and think about their special meaning for your life:

1. Romans 12:1-2
2. Colossians 3:1-4
3. I Corinthians 6:19-20
4. Galatians 2:20

It is a good idea to use this inventory at least once a year. But, whenever you find yourself struggling spiritually, do your 'checkup,' asking the Lord to reveal to you anything that might be causing your difficulties or feelings of spiritual weakness.

God's Promises and How to Claim Them

The Bible is filled with promises that God has made to His children. If you have not already done so, you should begin marking them in your Bible whenever you spot one. I suggest that you color code them to make them easier to find.[15] Your times of prayer should definitely include claiming God's promises. And be sure to spend time thanking Him for what He has promised. Here are a few examples of promises, and how to claim them in prayer. I suggest that you take time to memorize many of them. Having God's promises in your heart and mind will be an added blessing to your life.

I hope that you will spend the rest of your life finding and claiming these and many other words of promise from our Lord. They are written down for us to know and to claim!

Joshua 1:9 Have I not commanded you? Be strong and courageous. Do not be afraid; do not be discouraged, for the Lord your God will be with you wherever you go.

Lord, there are many things in my life that cause me to be discouraged and afraid. Because You promised to be with me wherever I am, I will be strong and courageous today, and obedient to Your will.

---

[15] A helpful resource for color-coding your Bible is available from amazon.com and lamplighters-ministries.org. It is: Color-Coding Your Bible by Cullinan and Sears. It is available as a digital download.

Psalm 100:3   Know that the LORD **is God. It is he who made us, and we are his; we are his people, the sheep of his pasture.**

Lord, I find great comfort in this promise: that I belong to you. I am just a sheep, but it is my joy to know and love you, my all-sufficient Shepherd. I count on You to meet all of my needs today. I love You, and I will gladly follow You wherever You lead me.

Psalm 55:22   Cast your cares on the LORD **and he will sustain you; he will never let the righteous be shaken.**

Dear Father, I confess that I tend to carry my own burdens and worries, instead of casting them onto You. Thank You for this reminder that You have promised to sustain me and care for me, helping me with everything that concerns me. Help me to find peace in that truth today, and every day.

Mark 9:23   "If you can?" said Jesus. "Everything is possible for one who believes."

Dear Lord, Help me to trust You today with all that concerns me. Help me to believe the truths that You have spoken in Your Word. Today I will believe truth, so that I will not hinder the working of Your Spirit in my life and circumstances.

Phil. 4:13 (Amp. N.T.) I can do all things [which He has called me to do] through Him who strengthens *and* empowers me [to fulfill His purpose—I am self-sufficient in Christ's sufficiency; I am ready for anything and equal to anything through Him who infuses me with inner strength and confident peace.]

What a joy, dear Father, to know that Your power gives me strength for anything I need! I cannot overcome my problems by my own strength, but I rely on Your empowerment today. I will lean on You.

Psalm 25:10 All the ways of the LORD are loving and faithful toward those who keep the demands of his covenant.

Dear Heavenly Father, I am so thankful that I do not ever need to be afraid of You, nor worried about what You might do to me. I realize that when I step out of the center of Your will, I can no longer be assured of Your greatest blessings. Please help me to walk closely to You, and to be obedient to Your will.

Phil. 4:6-7 Do not be anxious about anything, but in every situation, by prayer and petition, with thanksgiving, present your requests to God. And the peace of God, which transcends all understanding, will guard your hearts and your minds in Christ Jesus

Dear Lord Jesus, I need Your peace. Thank You that it is always available to me. Help me to remember that prayer is the key to unlocking the blessing of peace. And help me to wrap all of my prayers up in the garment of praise and thanksgiving.

Deut. 31:8 The Lord himself goes before you and will be with you; he will never leave you nor forsake you. Do not be afraid; do not be discouraged.

Dear Lord, I am so thankful for Your leadership in my life. Help me to remember this truth, especially when I begin to worry about the future. You are already there, walking before me and planning the way for me. Help me to remember to do my part in not allowing fear or discouragement to reside in my mind or heart.

Neh. 8:10b This day is holy to our Lord. Do not grieve, for the joy of the Lord is your strength.

Father God, sadness often engulfs my heart. Help me to remember the importance of focusing on You, the source of my true joy. And as joy fills my heart, I will have the strength I need to face life's challenges.

Romans 8:39 ··· neither height nor depth, nor anything else in all creation, will be able to separate us from the love of God that is in Christ Jesus our Lord.

Dear Father, I confess that sometimes I feel discouraged when a loved-one or friend hurts or betrays me. Thank You for the constancy of Your love, and for the peace that I experience when I open my heart to Your love.

John 8:12 When Jesus spoke again to the people, he said, "I am the light of the world. Whoever follows me will never walk in darkness, but will have the light of life."

Dear Heavenly Father, I confess that I sometimes walk in darkness, not knowing which way to turn. Help me to remember that You are my light as well as my guide. Remind me that if I remain in darkness, it is my fault, not Yours. Give me grace to walk with You; I never want to find myself engulfed in darkness.

Jere. 29:11 "For I know the plans I have for you," declares the Lord, "plans to prosper you and not to harm you, plans to give you hope and a future."

Precious Lord Jesus, it is such an encouragement to know that You have planned the best paths for me, and the best ways to experience Your blessings in my life. Help me to be open to Your guidance, watchful for how You are leading, and receptive to the blessings that You want to give to me.

Prov. 3:5-6 Trust in the LORD with all your heart and lean not on your own understanding; in all your ways submit to him, and he will make your paths straight.

Lord, I claim this promise, and I trust You to lead me on paths that are best for me. Help me to stop trying to figure out how You are working, but to simply trust You to control everything that concerns me. Help me to rest in this truth today.

I John 1:7 But if we walk in the light, as he is in the light, we have fellowship with one another, and the blood of Jesus, his Son, purifies us from all sin.

Lord, I thank you for this promise of forgiveness and cleansing. Help me to allow You to shine Your light on my life, and to allow You to show me anything that may be hindering my walk with You. And please, dear Lord, help me to learn to stay away from those people or things that lead me into sin, anything that will hinder my relationship with You.

Prov. 16:9 In their hearts humans plan their course, but the LORD establishes their steps.

What a precious promise from you, dear Lord. I can rely on You to guide me in the right paths. I know that You work in my life and circumstances each day; You want only what is best for me. Help me to cooperate with Your leadership today. I truly want to walk on the right paths that honor You.

James 1:5 If any of you lacks wisdom, you should ask God, who gives generously to all without finding fault, and it will be given to you.

Dear Lord, help me never to be afraid to come to You to ask for the wisdom You are so willing to give to Your child. I need to see my life and circumstances from Your perspective. Help me to stop trying to figure out the answers to what perplexes me, instead of asking You for Your wisdom.

---

2 Cor. 1:20 For no matter how many promises God has made, they are "Yes" in Christ. And so through him the "Amen" is spoken by us to the glory of God.

What a joy, dear Father, to know that every promise You have spoken in Your Word is meant for me to claim, since I belong to Your Son, Jesus. Help me to claim every one of them, and thus to glorify Your name. Thank You for Your love and faithfulness to me.

Ps 27:1 The LORD is my light and my salvation— whom shall I fear? The LORD is the stronghold of my life— of whom shall I be afraid?

Dear Heavenly Father, I am so thankful that I do not ever have to be afraid of anyone or anything. I gladly believe that You are in control of all that concerns me today and every day. You are my light in darkness, and my strength in weakness. I find my courage in You alone.

Rom. 8:28   And we know that in all things God works for the good of those who love him, who have been called according to his purpose.

Dear Lord Jesus, I find great peace and comfort in knowing that You are indeed in control of my life and circumstances. And even when things seem to go wrong for me, because of choices that I or others have made, I am so thankful that You are still at work to bring about good from it all!

Ps. 84:11   For the LORD God is a sun and shield; the LORD bestows favor and honor; no good thing does he withhold from those whose walk is blameless.

Dear Lord, I am so thankful for Your protection and blessings in my life. I know that Your desire is to bless Your child with all good things. Help me to walk faithfully with You, and to take care not to hinder our relationship. I do not want to disappoint You, or to keep You from revealing Your love to me, because of my sinful behavior.

Testimonies about Prayer

I put out word on Facebook and among other friends, asking them to write a short testimony of what prayer meant to them. Here are the results of that request:

James Lochridge: "Too often, I feel that Christians think prayer is coming to God with a laundry list of things that we want Him to do for us or our loved ones. They never spend any time listening for what God wants to share with them."

Ladell Shields: "This is how I feel about praying – it's a never-ending conversational presence with my best friend, Jesus."

Dee Tillett: "When your life changes because of prayer, then you will know how important it is and what it means."

Ercell Daves: "My mother used to say, 'If you're in the middle of a deep pond alone, keep paddling while you pray.'"

Brenda Morrison: "It is important to schedule an uninterrupted time with God each day."

Carol Richardson: "God should be our first resource, not our last resort. Prayer is sometimes lying at the feet of Jesus, ready to humbly receive God's will, even if it is not necessarily what you want."

Kim Williams Rudasill: "I like to begin praying with praise, and praying all through the day and when waking at night."

Angela Griffin Goode: "I try to include the phrase, 'I love you, Lord,' in my prayers."

Mary Charlotte Rodgerson: "Prayer is not as hard as some people think it is. Some of their misconceptions have robbed them of enjoying time with God. It is my daily source of wisdom, fellowship with Him and it is my lifeline. At least when I am NOT too busy and distracted by 'life' and my 'to do list' to remember to use it."

Christy Swink: "You can pray throughout the day, just like you'd talk to your best friend. It doesn't replace a quiet time with God, but we need to remember that praying doesn't have to be like a ritual."

Mellie Smith: "Prayer is how your heart knows God."

Elaine Ashley: "Having an attitude of prayer throughout the day is important."

Cindi Wood: "It is important to combine holiness with conversation praying.

Cindy Campos: "When I pray, I am always aware of His Spirit within me and just feel amazed that the Creator of the universe desires fellowship with ME! And as I've grown in my faith journey, I've come to long for and anticipate the time of fellowship we share together as I start my day with Him."

David Costner: "How do we get to know someone? We stand in their presence, give them our full attention, and converse with them. How do we become intimate with someone? We allow them into our hearts and minds, giving them the freedom to become a part of our very being. To have that kind of relationship with Almighty God, one must pray."

Jane Walton: "Standing on God's Word and exercising His Word in our prayer life is simply fundamental in our personal relationship with Jesus Christ as we journey with Him in our lives. He is teaching me more about listening, seeking Him, and just agreeing with Him in prayer. Oh, what a joy and exciting honor!"

Carolyn Reed: "We must pray BELIEVING God will answer. Believing puts us in the realm of faith. It is a choice we must make, just like choosing to believe Jesus forgives our sin."

Jay Washburn: "Prayer is talking to God, as well as listening to Him. It is building a relationship. It is most helpful when I am submissive to Him."

Jerry Wilkie: "I have the honor and privilege to be able to talk directly to my Creator any time, any day. I'm guaranteed He won't be out of town on business; He won't be on His cell phone' and He won't be too busy. No, I'm guaranteed that any time I pray, I have the Creator of the world's undivided attention. That makes me feel very special!"

Mattie Disher: " Prayer remains, after a morning start, as a thought process throughout my day. I believe prayer is about caring, sharing, and a gratitude attitude all day."

Gene Reymer: "Prayer should be an ongoing conversation with God, and we should let the smart one do most of the talking."

OTHER BOOKS

by

Dr. Alice R. Cullinan

Time for a Checkup: Assessing Our Progress in Spiritual Growth, published by CLC Publications.

Sorting it Out: Understanding God's Call to Ministry, published by Judson Press.

Books published by Lamplighters Ministries:[16]

Nuts and Bolts of Deacon Ministry, Cullinan and Dixon.

Furry Philosophy: What We Learned from our Four-Legged Friends, Cullinan and Sears.

Color-Coding Your Bible, Cullinan and Sears.

Widow Ministry, Cullinan

Joy in God's Presence (Devotional guide), Cullinan

Slaying Dragons: Dealing with Painful Emotions, Cullinan

Killer in the Camp: An Interactive Christian Mystery, Cullinan

Prayer: Common Questions and Misconceptions, Cullinan

---

[16] Available on amazon.com and lamplighters-ministries.org

Made in the USA
Monee, IL
07 June 2022